Island Treasures
Growing Up in Cuba

ALSO BY
ALMA FLOR ADA

The Gold Coin

I Love Saturdays y domingos

The Malachite Palace

My Name is María Isabel

Three Golden Oranges

The Unicorn of the West

Dear Peter Rabbit

Yours Truly, Goldilocks

With Love, Little Red Hen

Extra! Extra! Fairy-Tale News from Hidden Forest

BY ALMA FLOR ADA AND F. ISABEL CAMPOY

Tales Our Abuelitas Told: A Hispanic Folktale Collection

BY ALMA FLOR ADA AND GABRIEL M. ZUBIZARRETA

Dancing Home

Love, Amalia

Island Treasures
Growing Up in Cuba

Includes

Where the Flame Trees Bloom,
Under the Royal Palms
(winner of the Pura Belpré Award),

and the new collection
Days at La Quinta Simoni

Alma Flor Ada

Illustrations by Edel Rodriguez
and Antonio Martorell

ATHENEUM BOOKS FOR YOUNG READERS
New York London Toronto Sydney New Delhi

ATHENEUM BOOKS FOR YOUNG READERS
An imprint of Simon & Schuster Children's Publishing Division
1230 Avenue of the Americas, New York, New York 10020

This work is a memoir. It reflects the author's present recollections of her experiences over a period of years.

For information about special discounts for bulk purchases, please contact
Simon & Schuster Special Sales at 1-866-506-1949
or business@simonandschuster.com.
The Simon & Schuster Speakers Bureau can bring authors to your live event. For more
information or to book an event, contact the Simon & Schuster Speakers Bureau at
1-866-248-3049 or visit our website at www.simonspeakers.com.
Book design by Vikki Sheatsley and Lauren Rille
The text for this book is set in Adobe Garamond.
Manufactured in the United States of America
0715 FFG
First Edition
2 4 6 8 10 9 7 5 3 1
Library of Congress Cataloging-in-Publication Data
Ada, Alma Flor.
[Memoirs. Selections]
Island treasures : growing up in Cuba : includes Where the flame trees bloom, Under the
royal palms, and five brand new stories / Alma Flor Ada ; illustrations by Antonio Martorell.
— First edition.
pages cm
ISBN 978-1-4814-4245-9 (hc)
ISBN 978-1-4814-2900-9 (pbk)
ISBN 978-1-4814-5891-7 (eBook)
1. Ada, Alma Flor—Childhood and youth—Juvenile literature. 2. Authors, American—20th
century—Biography—Juvenile literature. 3. Authors, Cuban—20th century—Biography—
Juvenile literature. 4. Ada, Alma Flor—Homes and haunts—Cuba—Juvenile literature.
5. Cuban American women—Biography—Juvenile literature. 6. Cuba—Social life and
customs—Juvenile literature. 7. Cuba—Intellectual life—Juvenile literature. 8. Families—
Cuba—Juvenile literature. I. Martorell, Antonio, 1939- illustrator. II. Ada, Alma Flor.
Where the flame trees bloom. III. Ada, Alma Flor. Under the royal palms. IV. Title.
PS3551.D22A6 2015
813'.54—dc23
2014034812

Island Treasures
Growing Up in Cuba

Contents

*One of my first photos
I was 47 days old*

Bath time

With my aunt Lolita's guitar

A Note from the Author

ISLAND TREASURES contains two previously published books—
Where the Flame Trees Bloom (1998) and *Under the Royal Palms*
(2000)—as well as *Days at La Quinta Simoni,* a set of stories
new to this collection. All of these narratives are based on my
childhood memories.

Writing about my childhood has been a way of keeping
alive cherished memories and honoring the people who nourished me. Today, there is another reason I treasure these stories:
the response they have received, over the last fifteen years, from
readers who have found delight and inspiration in their pages.

Many of you have written to tell me that the attention these
stories give to the simple details of daily life has helped you
value things previously taken for granted. Others have written
to say that these stories moved you to a greater appreciation of
your own families. And I am delighted whenever I hear that
some of you have begun to write about your own lives!

It is my hope that, through my recollections of everyday
moments, new readers of all ages and from all over the planet
will come to understand this unique period in Cuban life—
and to discover that each one of us has a world of stories to tell.

Where the Flame Trees Bloom

with illustrations by Edel Rodriguez
and Antonio Martorell

*To Samantha Rose
as your life begins to bloom*

Introduction

A Ceiba or Kapok tree

A Royal Palm tree

I WAS BORN IN Cuba. The largest of the islands in the Caribbean, Cuba is long and narrow. If one looks at a map of Cuba with a little bit of imagination, the island resembles a giant alligator, resting on the water. The western part of Cuba is very near Florida, while the eastern part is very close to the Dominican Republic and Haiti. In climate and natural beauty, Cuba is quite similar to Puerto Rico. In fact, Cubans and Puerto Ricans have a shared history, which is why a Puerto Rican poet once said that "Cuba and Puerto Rico are two wings of one bird."

On both ends and also in the center, Cuba has high mountain ranges covered with dense tropical forests. In between these three mountainous regions are flat, fertile lands. I grew up on the eastern plains, the cattle region, on the outskirts of Camagüey. Ours was a town of brick houses with tile roofs and massive old churches built of stone, which in the past served both as houses of worship and refuge for pirates. The churches' high towers allowed lookouts to keep watch for cattle-thieving buccaneers.

The house I was born in, La Quinta Simoni, was very large and very old. My *abuelita* Lola, my mother's mother, had inherited it from her father. My youngest aunt, Lolita, had been born in the house. A generation later, two of my younger cousins (Nancy and Mireyita), my sister Flor, and I were also born in the same house—right at home, not in a hospital.

Although the house was large, we were not wealthy. However, I did grow up surrounded by a wealth of family. At one time, grandparents, aunts, uncles, and cousins all lived together under one roof. For one wonderful year, my two older cousins, Jorge and Virginita, also lived there. Yet for most of the first seven years of my childhood, I was the only child living in the house.

La Quinta Simoni also held a lot of history. It was originally built as a colonial *hacienda*, or ranch, by an Italian family, the Simoni. Life on their *hacienda* included planting crops, raising cattle, and tanning hides, as well as making bricks, tiles, and household vessels from the red clay found by the river. In those days, most of the work was done by the people the Simoni kept as slaves.

Much later, by the time I was a child, the house had grown old and weathered and the gardens overgrown. The central fountain, now dry and filled with earth, served as a planter for ferns. In the back of the house, several large rooms that had once served as dormitories for the enslaved workers were now put to other uses. A short distance away, a small brick house called *el calabozo* stood as a reminder of the horrible things human beings can do to one another; the iron rings on its walls had been meant to hold people in chains.

During colonial times, one of the two daughters of the Simoni family, Amalia, married Ignacio Agramonte, a Cuban patriot who fought to gain independence and freedom for all who live in Cuba. One of the first acts of the Cuban Revolution in 1868 was to free all slaves.

It was this connection with the Cuban struggle for freedom, not its earlier painful history, that made my family proud of our home. For me, the past was filled with unanswerable questions: How could anyone dare to think that a person could be owned by another? And how could we be so proud of our freedom and independence while some children still walked the streets barefoot and hungry?

Even with these troublesome questions—big ones for a young child to ponder—the old house remained a magical world for me. In addition to large flocks of chickens, ducks, and geese, my *abuelita* kept peacocks as well. The colorful birds often perched in the open dining room windows that faced out into the garden. Sometimes they would nest atop a large masonry arch, built as a small-scale replica of the French *Arc de Triomphe* in the long-abandoned garden by the river. Bats hid above the porch ceiling, and doves flocked on the terraces. My mother took in every stray cat that crossed her path, and the garden and courtyard were busy with lizards and snails, frogs and toads, crickets and grasshoppers. A family of hawks lived in the branches of a nearby tree. Yet even among all these living wonders, my best friends were the trees.

Large, firm, and strong, the trees offered me their friendship in many different ways. Their green canopies provided treasured shade during the heat of the day, allowing me to stay outdoors while sheltered from the tropical sun. Whether I felt lonely or joyful, they always welcomed me.

Ancient flame trees, more than a hundred years old, formed an avenue along one side of the house leading to the white arch and the river. Gnarled with age, their large roots protruded from the earth, offering me a nest where I could crawl in to feel protected and secure. Their worn, smooth roots were pleasant to the touch, and I would caress them as one might hold a dear friend's hand.

The old river Tínima, winding its way through the land, had formed a rather large island behind the house. Long ago, the island had been planted with fruit trees. Now the mature trees were generous with their offerings, better than any store-bought candy or even any dessert made in our kitchen. Sweet and sour *tamarindos*, which made a refreshing drink when soaked in water; fragrant *guayabas*, brilliantly green outside with a sweet red inside; *caimitos*, round as baseballs, with a shining purple skin and a delicate, milky-white flesh; bittersweet *marañones*, vivid bells of deep yellow or red, each one with a delicious nut hanging below: the cashews that my uncle Medardito and my young aunt Lolita loved to roast over a campfire by the river.

And then there were the dozens of coconut trees, with fronds that swayed in the breeze and fruits that we treasured above all others. The water of the young *cocos* is sweet and fresh. As the coconut matures, the water inside slowly turns dense and smooth like a light gelatin. Later it becomes fleshier, but still soft and sweet. We loved to eat these treats right out of their shells. As coconuts age, their meat becomes hard and dry; it can then be shredded to make desserts. But the most highly valued kind of coconut treat took much longer to form. If a large, healthy coconut was kept at the right temperature in a moist and dark place, then perhaps it would sprout. If it did, and if someone knew how to open it at the right time, she would find that the thick, dry meat inside had pulled away from the shell and had gathered in the very center of the coconut as a soft, porous ball, the deliciously sweet *"manzana del coco"* or "coconut apple."

On the shore of our river island stood a bamboo grove. There, my *abuelita* Lola hung her hammock every afternoon, to rest a while between her two jobs. Rustling through the bamboo and the coconut palms, the wind would play a soothing, enchanting melody that soon lulled her to sleep. Although we lived inland, a few hours from the seashore, this sound reminded me of an ocean breeze, filled with rumors of distant lands and far-away places.

While I grew up surrounded by loving people and fascinated by all the life around me, it was to the trees that I chose to tell my sorrows and my joys, and most of all, my dreams.

Like a family, the trees grew and their branches multiplied.

Some, like the flame trees, were stolid and almost timeless. Others were abundant with fruit and offspring. Each, in its own way, mirrored the life around me—the life that is now reflected in these pages.

The family stories you are about to read took place at various times. Some happened before I was born and were told to me as a child; others happened to me as I was growing up. Most of them took place at La Quinta Simoni, the magnificent old house of my early childhood; others in town, where we moved when I was eight. But even then, I was fortunately never too far away from my beloved trees.

As I share these stories with you now, I can still see the tall and majestic royal palms, the graceful coconut trees swaying easily in the warm tropical breezes, and the fiery flame trees, bursting all over with their abundant red blossoms. And I hope that the inspiration I continue to receive from these companions of my childhood will, in turn, help warm the hearts of those who turn the pages of this book.

Chapter 1

The Teacher

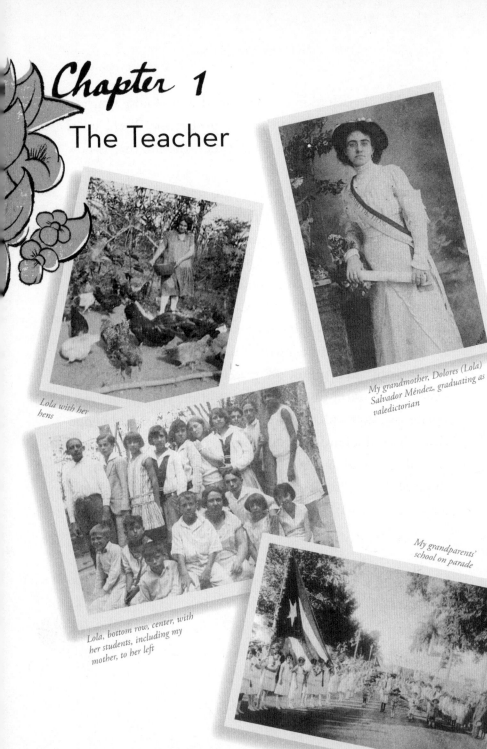

Lola with her hens

My grandmother, Dolores (Lola) Salvador Méndez, graduating as valedictorian

Lola, bottom row, center, with her students, including my mother, to her left

My grandparents' school on parade

My MOTHER'S MOTHER, my grandmother Dolores, was known as Lola. She filled my early years with outdoor adventures, fun, and fascinating stories. The deeds of the Greek gods and goddesses, the heroic feats of the Cuban patriots—these were as immediate to me as her everyday life at the two schools where she was principal: an elementary public school during the day, and a school for working women in the evenings.

It is not surprising that there are many stories in our family about this woman who was both an intellectual and a practical person, who cut her hair and shortened her skirts before any other woman in our town, who created a literary journal, founded schools, awakened a great passion in the poet who married her, and brought up five children as well as several nieces and nephews while directing her own schools and farm.

One of my favorite stories about her was told to me at various times by my mother and by my aunts Mireya and Virginia, since all three of them were present when the events took place. Unlike many other family stories, which are often changed or embellished depending on the teller, I have always heard this story told exactly the same way. Perhaps that is because the story itself is too powerful to be embellished, or because the events impressed themselves so vividly upon the memories of those present.

Abuelita Lola loved to teach outdoors. The slightest pretext would serve to take the whole class out under the trees to conduct her lessons there. This particular story took place during one of those outdoor lessons, at a time when she and her husband, abuelito Medardo, ran a boarding school at La Quinta Simoni on the *hacienda* she had inherited from her father (and where I would later be born).

Surrounded by her pupils, including three of her own daughters, my grandmother was conducting a grammar lesson. Suddenly she interrupted herself. "Why is it," she asked her students, "that we don't often speak about the things that are truly important? About our responsibility as human beings for those around us? Do we really know their feelings, their needs? And yet we could all do so much for each other. . . ."

The students were silent, spellbound. They knew their teacher sometimes strayed from the topic of the lesson in order to share with them her own reflections. And they also knew that those were some of her most important lessons. At times she could be funny and witty. Other times, she would touch their hearts. And so they listened.

"Look," continued my grandmother, as she pointed to the road that bordered the farm. There the students saw a solitary man walking. "Look at that old man. He is walking by us. In a few minutes he will be gone forever, and we will never have known who he is, where he is going, what may be important in his life."

The students watched the man, who by then was quite close. He was very thin, and a coarse *guayabera* hung loosely over his bent frame. His face, in the shade of a straw hat, was weathered and wrinkled.

"Well," said my grandmother, "do we let him go away, forever unknown, or do you want to ask him if there is anything we can do for him?"

The students looked at one another. Finally one girl said: "Shall I ask him?" As my grandmother nodded, the girl got up and walked toward the road. A few of the other students followed her, my mother and my aunts among them.

Upon seeing them approach, the man stopped. "We would like to know who you are, and where you are going," said the student. "Is there anything we can do for you?" added my aunt Mireya.

The man was completely taken aback. "But, who are *you*?" was all he could reply.

The girls then explained how their questions had come about. The old man looked at them. He told them that he had no one to be with, that he had come a long distance hoping to find some distant relatives, but had been unable to locate them. "I'm nothing but an old man," he concluded, "looking for a place to lie down and die. As a matter of fact, I was heading toward that large *ceiba*." He pointed to a large tree growing by

the road not too far away. "I thought I'd lie down in its shade to wait for my death."

"Please don't leave" was all the girls could say. They rushed back to tell their teacher what they had learned from the old man, that he truly intended to just lie down and die.

"What do you think can be done?" my grandmother asked. The boys and girls came up with ideas: The old man could go to an old folks' home. Maybe he should be taken to the hospital, or perhaps the police would know what to do. . . . "Is that what you would like to happen, if it were you?" my grandmother asked.

Instead, the children took the man into the house. He was given a room. The students made the bed and cooked him some food. A doctor determined that there was nothing wrong with him except exhaustion and malnutrition. It took him several days to recuperate, but soon he was up and about. He lived on with the family for many years, until one morning he was found to have died peacefully in his sleep. During all those years, he helped in the garden, fed the hens, and often sat on the back porch, whistling softly. But there was nothing he liked better than to sit in the back of the classroom, or out under the trees, and listen to my grandmother teach.

Chapter 2
Choices

From left to right: me; my sister, Flor; my grandfather Modesto Ada Barral; my father, Modesto Ada Rey; my mother, Alma; and my uncle Mario

MY FATHER'S FAMILY and my mother's family were as different from each other as a quiet mountain stream and the vast ocean. My father's family was small in contrast to my mother's, with its many aunts, uncles, first and second cousins, great-aunts, and great-uncles. But not only was my mother's family large, it also was very lively, cheerful, and adventurous, while my father's father and brothers were quiet people who seldom spoke about anything personal.

We frequently spent our evenings together listening to stories of my mother's family. Through these stories people whom I had never met seemed as familiar to me as those who lived nearby. It seemed as though I had heard their voices and taken part in their adventures. But it is a story told to me by my father's father that I would like to share with you now, a story that remains vivid in my memory and that has greatly shaped who I am today.

Abuelito Modesto would stop by my house every afternoon for a short visit, always with a cigarette between his yellowed fingers. He would pat me on the head or give me a formal kiss on the forehead, and then he would sit and talk with my parents about the political and social issues of the day. He sounded very knowledgeable to me, but also adult and remote. He was a large, formidable man, and although I listened in fascination to his words, I felt as if it would be many years before I would be able to share anything with him, or he with me.

One afternoon when he arrived, my parents had gone out and I was the only one at home. He sat to wait for them in the dining room, the coolest room in the city house where we lived at the time. The house was bathed in the quiet so prevalent in the tropics during the hottest part of the day. As usual, I was buried in a book. Then abuelito Modesto called my name and motioned for me to sit on his lap. I was surprised by this gesture of warmth and affection, since I was almost ten years old and especially since he never asked any of us to sit by him. Yet I welcomed the invitation to get close to this man who seemed so remote and yet so wise. I never knew what prompted him to tell me the story that came next, but I have always treasured it.

"You probably know that I was once very wealthy," he began. As I nodded, he continued. "I was only twelve years old when I left Spain to come to Cuba. My father had died, and since my oldest brother was arrogant and very authoritarian, I decided to leave my home at La Coruña. I roamed the port until someone pointed out a ship that was about to sail, and I managed to hide aboard. A sailor discovered me shortly after the ship set sail, but the captain said I should sail with them, and when we arrived at Havana he helped me get

ashore. I searched for work, and fortunately I was taken in by the owner of a hardware store. He worked me hard! I cleaned the store and helped with all kinds of odd jobs. I had to sleep in the storage room on some burlap sacks, but I learned the business well.

"One day a young American came into the store with a surprising machine that played music from round black disks. It was made in the United States and was called a gramophone. I was astonished and excited. Imagine, a machine that could bring the great opera singer Enrico Caruso's voice into each home! The hardware store owner didn't want anything to do with this machine, but I was fascinated by it. I followed the American when he left the store and offered to work for him. For the next few years, I sold this new invention. Eventually I became the major representative in Cuba for RCA, the manufacturer, and traveled the island from end to end. I loved the land around Camagüey, and I saw how cattle could thrive on these fertile plains, so I bought some land. The land turned out to be even more valuable than I thought, and I became wealthy."

He paused. Even though I didn't know then the meaning of the word *nostalgia,* I know now that is exactly what I saw in his eyes. "The years passed," he continued. "I married your grandmother and we had four sons. Then she became very ill. Since she was too ill to be moved, I had a doctor come to the *hacienda.* But although he did all he could, she did not improve.

"One evening, an exhausted horse and rider galloped up to

the *hacienda*. The rider was my business manager in Havana. He'd ridden at top speed from the train station in Camagüey, and close up, I saw that it was not only exhaustion that marked his face, but panic. 'You must come to Havana immediately,' he urged me. 'There is a financial crisis and the economy is collapsing. The president of your bank sent me to warn you. It's urgent that you travel to the capital in person to withdraw all of your money, or else it will be lost.' I considered his alarming news as the man looked at me impatiently, unable to understand why I wasn't ordering fresh horses to take us to the train. But was I to leave your ill grandmother?"

He paused again, and I saw that the look in his eyes had changed. This new feeling was one I recognized even as a child. My own eyes must have looked the same the day I found a bird, which only a short while ago had been alive, lying dead in our backyard.

My grandfather finished his story: "I did not return with him. Your grandmother did not get well, and the economy did collapse before I could get my money from the bank. I was no longer a rich man. But I was there by your grandmother's side until the end, and I held her hand in mine as she passed away." I looked down at my grandfather's big hand, which was covering my own. And then I knew I would not have to wait until I grew up to understand my grandfather Modesto.

There is no one alive today who remembers María Rey Paz, the grandmother I never knew. And there are probably very few people living who remember my quiet but steadfast grandfather, Modesto. Yet I am certain that these ancestors of mine live on in my children, who have known from a young age what choices to make where loved ones are concerned.

Chapter 3

The Surveyor

My father, Modesto

My FATHER, NAMED Modesto after his father, was a surveyor. Some of the happiest times of my childhood were spent on horseback, on trips where he would allow me to accompany him as he plotted the boundaries of small farms in the Cuban countryside. Sometimes we slept out under the stars, stringing our hammocks between the trees, and drank fresh water from springs. We always stopped for a warm greeting at the simple huts of the neighboring peasants, and my eyes would drink in the lush green forest crowned by the swaying leaves of the palm trees.

Since many surveying jobs called for dividing up land that a family had inherited from a deceased parent or relative, my father's greatest concern was that justice be achieved. It was not enough just to divide the land into equal portions. He also had to ensure that all parties would have access to roads, to water sources, to the most fertile soil. While I was able to join him on some trips, other surveying work involved large areas of land. On these jobs, my father was part of a team, and I would stay home, eagerly waiting to hear the stories from his trip on his return.

Latin-American families tend not to limit their family boundaries to those who are born or have married into it. Any good friend who spends time with the family and shares in its daily experiences is welcomed as a member. The following story from one of my father's surveying trips is not about a member of my blood family, but instead concerns a member of our extended family.

Félix Caballero, a man my father always liked to recruit whenever he needed a team, was rather different from the other surveyors. He was somewhat older, unmarried, and he kept his thoughts to himself. He came to visit our house daily. Once there, he would sit silently in one of the living room's four rocking chairs, listening to the lively conversations all around him. An occasional nod or a single word were his only contributions to those conversations. My mother and her sisters sometimes made fun of him behind his back. Even though they never said so, I had the impression that they questioned why my father held him in such high regard.

Then one day my father shared this story.

"We had been working on foot in mountainous country for most of the day. Night was approaching. We still had a long way to go to return to where we had left the horses, so we decided to cut across to the other side of the mountain, and soon found ourselves facing a deep gorge. The gorge was spanned by a railroad bridge, long and narrow, built for the sugarcane trains. There were no side rails or walkways, only a set of tracks resting on thick, heavy crossties suspended high in the air.

"We were all upset about having to climb down the steep gorge and up the other side, but the simpler solution, walking across the bridge, seemed too dangerous. What if a cane train should appear? There would be nowhere to go. So we all began the long descent . . . all except for Félix. He decided to risk walking across the railroad bridge. We all tried to dissuade him, but to no avail. Using an old method, he put one ear to the tracks to listen for vibrations. Since he heard none, he decided that no train was approaching. So he began to cross the long bridge, stepping from crosstie to crosstie between the rails, balancing his long red-and-white surveyor's poles on his shoulder.

"He was about halfway across the bridge when we heard the ominous sound of a steam engine. All eyes rose to Félix. Unquestionably he had heard it too, because he had stopped in the middle of the bridge and was looking back.

"As the train drew closer, and thinking there was no other solution, we all shouted: 'Jump! Jump!', not even sure our voices would carry up to where he stood, so high above us. Félix did look down at the rocky riverbed, which, as it was the dry season, held little water. We tried to encourage him with gestures and more shouts, but he had stopped looking down. We could not imagine what he was doing next, squatting on the tracks, with the engine of the train already visible. And then, we understood. . . .

"Knowing that he could not manage to hold on to the thick wooden crossties, Félix laid his thin but resilient surveyor's poles across the ties, parallel to the rails. Then he let his body slip down between two of the ties, as he held on to

the poles. And there he hung, below the bridge, suspended over the gorge but safely out of the train's path.

"The cane train was, as they frequently are, a very long train. To us, it seemed interminable. . . . One of the younger men said he counted two hundred and twenty cars. With the approaching darkness, and the smoke and shadows of the train, it was often difficult to see our friend. We had heard no human sounds, no screams, but would we have heard anything at all, with the racket of the train crossing overhead?

"When the last car began to curve around the mountain, we could just make out Félix's lonely figure still hanging beneath the bridge. We all watched in relief and amazement as he pulled himself up and at last finished walking, slowly and calmly, along the tracks to the other side of the gorge."

After I heard that story, I saw Félix Caballero in a whole new light. He still remained as quiet as ever, prompting a smile from my mother and her sisters as he sat silently in his rocking chair. But in my mind's eye, I saw him crossing that treacherous bridge, stopping to think calmly of what to do to save his life, emerging all covered with soot and smoke but triumphantly alive—a lonely man, hanging under a railroad bridge at dusk, suspended from his surveyor's poles over a rocky gorge.

If there was so much courage, such an ability to calmly confront danger in the quiet, aging man who sat rocking in our living room, what other wonders might lie hidden in every human soul?

Chapter 4
Lightning

My uncle Mario; me, on my first birthday, standing on top of my aunt Mireya;
and my mother, Alma

MARIO, MY FATHER'S younger brother, was a teacher in the countryside. To get to his school he had to take the train and then ride for a few hours on horseback.

The school was housed in a *bohío*, a country hut built of rough wooden planks and a thatched roof made from guano palm fronds. The students sat on benches—three, four, or when attendance was especially good, even five to a bench. But attendance was seldom good. In the countryside, girls often stayed home to help with their little brothers and sisters, to do the washing, and to gather wood for the stove. Boys often missed school because they had to help in the fields, planting, weeding, or harvesting. For the most part, the *campesinos* did not believe that schooling would do much to improve their children's lives, and therefore did not see a compelling reason for them to attend.

My uncle came back to the city every Friday night, tired, exhausted, and somewhat depressed. "What's the use?" I often heard him say. Soon he too cut class whenever possible.

Often, on Monday, he would procrastinate and miss the train. An upset stomach or a small cold was reason enough not to travel. Many times he went on Tuesday, and the week would be only four days long. Other times he came back on Thursday night. "Attendance was poor this week," he would say. "It always gets worse on Friday, so I just came home."

My father never criticized him. Ever since their mother had died when my father was fifteen and my uncle only ten, my father had taken care of Mario. I think the painful memory of their shared loss, their unhappiness at having been sent to boarding school, the loneliness they had both felt, gave my father compassion for his brother. Although Mario was now a man, my father continued to indulge and protect him. My mother, on the other hand, constantly chided my uncle. "How are the children ever going to value their education when you yourself don't? You could do so much for them. . . ."

Tío Mario was a person of few words. He drew back from arguments, turning beet red whenever he was teased, and never tried to defend himself. In fact, he seldom spoke much at all.

I could see my uncle's predicament. We were his only family, and, I suspect, his only friends. It must have been hard to have my mother always reprimanding him, but he just kept silent, and continued to spend his weekends with us.

But one Friday night, tío Mario did not make his usual appearance at dinner. More surprisingly, he had still not returned by Saturday night, nor on Sunday. My mother asked my father, my father asked my grandfather, but no one seemed to know where he was.

Nor did we see or hear from him the following week. Everyone wondered and speculated and worried. There had been heavy rains, so maybe the rivers had flooded and he had been unable to get across. After all, he had often used this excuse in order to avoid going back to school on Monday. Perhaps this time it had really happened after all.

The next weekend arrived but there was still no news of my uncle. Although my father became increasingly alarmed, there was no telephone or telegraph that could reach the remote countryside where the school was.

Three weeks later, when tío Mario finally returned, he looked like a different man. His normally pink skin was tanned, and his carefully polished nails were now broken and dirty. He needed a haircut. But for the first time ever, he looked sunburned and strong.

He said nothing at all about his absence, and as if by agreement, no one else mentioned it either. We all sat down to lunch.

We were enjoying the black beans and rice, the sweet fried plantains, when I noticed on my uncle's wrist a dark yellow scab, where he normally wore his wristwatch.

"Tío, what is that?" I couldn't help but ask.

"Oh, that . . . It's from lightning."

There was a moment of silence. My mother set down the pitcher of coconut water, even though her glass was still empty. My father put down his fork and knife. No one said a word. At last my uncle spoke.

"That first week I was gone," my uncle said slowly, "there was a very big storm." And then he stopped.

"And?" prompted my father. "What about the lightning?"

"The lightning was everywhere," my uncle continued. "It was difficult to teach above the noise of the thunder. The lightning bolts seemed to be flashing all around us. . . ." And then he stopped again.

"Were many children present?" my mother asked.

And as if this were the very cue he needed, my uncle resumed the story:

"Yes, for once, they were all present. It was crowded and hot in that small room. And the children were all excited, as if charged by the storm. And then, it happened. . . ."

We all held still, waiting to hear what came next.

"I didn't even hear the thunder when lightning struck the large mango tree next to the school. I simply passed out. When I awoke, I felt an intense pain in my arm. My watch had melted right onto my wrist. But I didn't pay attention to it. All of the children were strewn about the floor. Every single one of them . . ."

"Were they dead?" There was panic in my mother's voice.

"That's what I thought when I first saw them. 'Here they are, all dead,' I said to myself. 'All because they came to hear a teacher who doesn't even believe in their future.' But little by little, they began to stir. Thank goodness no one was hurt. They weren't even scared. But I, I was. . . ."

"So that's why you didn't come all this time . . . ," said my father, more to himself than to my uncle.

"I've been working on the school. I asked some of the fathers to help me enlarge it. And we are building more benches. We also made a larger blackboard. It will take a while before everything is in place. I spoke with one of the families about renting a room, because I am turning my old room next to the classroom into an art workshop. There is so much to be done, I'll probably be coming back only once a month to get supplies."

My mother poured herself a large glass of coconut water. As she lifted it to her lips, a golden ray of light came in through the dining room window and lit up the glass. It looked as though she were making an offering.

Chapter 5

Samoné

Ceiba tree
planted by my
grandmother

Río Tinima at La Quinta Simoni

Dark clouds had covered the sky all day. I was sitting in the window seat of a large front window that reached almost to the floor, looking down the road and waiting for the rain. Would there be a storm with bolts of lightning? If so, I would not be allowed to go outside; but if it was a peaceful tropical rain, I would be able to put on my bathing suit and run outdoors into the garden, under the trees. I loved to stand under their canopies and let the water drip down on me from their leaves. How fresh and fragrant was the water that filtered through the orange and lemon trees!

Just then I saw the man approaching. He was tall and burly, with an unkempt beard, large, bushy eyebrows, and well-tanned, weathered skin. He had a burlap sack on his shoulder, and I was surprised to see him turn toward our house. When he knocked on the door I was scared. Instead of calling my mother or one of my aunts, I went in search of my father.

"I'm looking for work," were the man's first words. "And I can do anything . . . plant, weed, feed the chickens, tend the horses, milk the cows."

My father didn't reply. I knew we weren't looking for anyone. La Quinta Simoni was not a true *hacienda* anymore. We kept hardly any animals, and we certainly didn't need anyone to feed my grandmother's chickens and peacocks. But the man was determined to let us know all that he could do.

"I can make charcoal . . . and you seem to have plenty of *marabú.*" He was right. The thorny plant that could be converted into charcoal had taken over most of the fallow farmland.

"It won't cost you much. Just a place to stay and something to eat," he said, and then he looked at me. A broad smile lit his face. "And I know plenty of stories to tell the little girl. . . ."

I saw my father return his smile. He was not sure about needing to make charcoal, but he would find something for this man to do.

Samoné had spoken truly. Work seemed to be his life, and he was very good at everything he did. He was up before sunrise, and except for a brief pause for a cup of coffee and a quick lunch, he worked until sundown. Soon Samoné had become part of the family.

The farm began to show the fruits of his care. Where there had only been weeds before, now there was a vegetable garden. The hens seemed to lay more eggs, pleased with the fresh-cut *canutillo* grass he brought them from the river. There were more chicks, more geese.

But best of all, every evening after dinner, Samoné shared with us the one gift he had not mentioned, and music filled the air. He sat outside, leaning against a wall on a sturdy *taburete*— a rustic chair with a cowhide back and seat—and played his

accordion. Although his speaking voice was deep and strong, I never heard him sing. Instead, he would hum softly to himself as he played. It was the accordion that sang for him: sad, melancholy tangos, sweet boleros, lively polkas, enchanting *habaneras*.

Just as he worked without pause during the day, at night Samoné played without stopping. He played while my mother helped me undress and get into my pajamas. He played while my father told me bedtime stories. And he would still be playing as I lay quietly in bed, trying to not fall asleep so that I could continue listening as the music came in through my window, bathed in the fragrance of jasmine. . . .

Samoné had been with us for a couple of years when he again suggested that he make some charcoal. My father tried to dissuade him, saying that it was too much work and too dangerous, hardly worth the amount of effort it demanded. But Samoné was determined to start his own furnaces.

To make the coal, it was first necessary to cut *marabú* bushes, and then to strip the thorny branches until only the trunk remained, clean as a stick. These sticks were then propped up, as if to form a tepee. When several layers of sticks were in place, they were covered with dirt, leaving only a small opening through which to ignite the wood. The strong wood would burn slow and hot over a period of days, turning gradually into charcoal.

It was important that the charcoal maker watch the *horno de carbón*, the charcoal oven, day and night. Sometimes, if one had not been sealed correctly, it would burst into flames. Other times, if the green wood contained too much sap, it could explode.

Samoné, however, never got to guard his furnace. While he was cutting through the thorny *marabú* bushes, his machete got caught on a rebellious branch, slipped out of his hand, and came slashing down on his right arm.

It was almost Christmas when it happened. My mother and I had been decorating our small tree. I sat in the front window seat, alternately looking inside at the beautiful tree and outside at a group of boys who were flying kites in the open field across the road.

Suddenly Samoné staggered in and almost fell. He left a bright crimson trail behind him.

"¡Mamá!" I screamed, grateful that she was so close at hand.

A passing car stopped to drive Samoné and my mother to the hospital. As they drove away, she held his arm still with towels that were already as red as carnations.

For weeks, only Samoné's burly fingers, purple and inflamed, poked out from his bandaged arm. Unable to work, Samoné himself walked around in a daze. The only thing that livened him up a bit was bringing fresh grass to the hens. As he could only use one hand, even this simple task now took him most of the day.

I couldn't wait for the day that the bandage would come off. But when it was finally removed, and the ugly scar along his arm was laid bare, Samoné discovered that he could not get his hand to respond. He could not close his fingers, nor could they hold any weight.

My uncle gave Samoné a rubber ball and encouraged him to try to hold it in his hand, to try to close his fingers around it. It was heartbreaking to see the ball fall again and again. Samoné did not give up, and would sit on the porch for hours with the ball, but he looked embarrassed and ashamed as the ball continued to fall.

Since the accident, there had been no accordion music at night. Now that the bandages had come off, the nightly silence felt even more oppressive to me. I began to go to the river with Samoné to help him bring in the grass. Before, whenever we had spent time together, he had told me stories about bright rabbits and nasty foxes. Yet now all that I heard from him were heavy sighs. It was as though the purpose in his life had left him, drained out through the hand he could no longer use.

Then Samoné began to disappear in the afternoons. No one knew where he went. Nobody said much about it, but I could see worried looks on my mother's face when he began to skip dinner too. Sometimes, when he was gone, I felt as though I heard an echo of his music.

Then one night, when I was already in bed, I did hear it. Somewhat tentative, and not as bright as it had been before, but there it was: the beautiful sound of a *guajira,* a gentle love

song from the Cuban countryside. Samoné, practicing tena-
ciously in solitude, had found a way to create music again.

I jumped out of bed, tiptoed into the dining room, and
looked out into the courtyard. There he was, poised somewhat
awkwardly on his *taburete,* opening and closing the accordion
with his knees while he played the keys with his left hand. Yet
the music sounded soft and clear, accompanied by Samoné's
familiar hum, while the rays of moonlight, filtering through
the branches of the flame trees, shone upon the smile that lit
his face.

Chapter 6

The Legend

A fruit tree in Emilio Pimentel's orchard

Me with Emilio Pimentel, 90 years old, and his family

The altar in Emilio's house

I HAVE ALWAYS LOVED legends and stories that relate mysterious events. There were many legends connected to our old house, La Quinta Simoni. People said that there was a buried treasure somewhere on the land, and that ghosts were seen at night trying to find it. Some swore that the spirits of former slaves could be heard crying at night. Others were convinced that they had seen the ghost of Ignacio Agramonte, the patriot from the Cuban War for Independence who had once lived in the house, riding his horse through the fields at night. We knew that what people mistook for a white horse was really the white arch which stood far behind the house, in the abandoned garden next to the river. As for the other ghosts, we ourselves had never seen nor heard them. But on one occasion, I actually had the chance to witness a legend being born—though at the time it happened, I did not realize how enduring a legend it would be.

Our house stood on the outskirts of town, far away from any other except for the tiny house where my great-grandmother lived. At night, a few lights shone dimly on the stretch of road right in front of the house. Otherwise, the darkness was complete.

As the road curved out away from town, it passed by the army headquarters. A little further still, it reached a cluster of simple shacks. To shorten their way to town, the people who lived there had cut some trails through the thorny *marabú* bushes that covered most of the neglected fields behind our house. But these trails were not only being used as a shortcut. Thieves had begun to frequent the trails at night.

One night, a hen was stolen; the next, clothes from the clothes line, a spade, a bucket, or a wheelbarrow. Things were constantly disappearing, and each time it seemed as if the thieves were getting bolder.

The thieves had their big night after *Día de Reyes*, a feast celebrated on January 6 when children in Cuba receive their holiday gifts. My uncle Medardito's new watch, which he had placed upon his nightstand; my cousin Jorge's new bicycle; my own *carriola*, the scooter that I had longed for: all had disappeared by the morning after the holiday.

"This is too much," the family agreed. "Things have gone too far."

"We need to put a stop to the thievery," said my uncle.

"But what can we do?" asked one of my aunts.

"I have an idea," proposed my father. His plan was that he and my uncle would walk down the trails toward the shacks in the middle of the night. Halfway there, my father would shoot his revolver into the air a few times. "Maybe that will frighten the thieves away, by letting them know we are armed."

Over the next few days, I heard repeated accounts of the events that had been set in motion by my father's plan. My uncle and he had indeed set out that night. As they began to walk toward the village, Samoné, our hired worker, decided to join them.

The three of them made their way with a flashlight, not always succeeding at steering clear of the thornbushes. When they were halfway across the fields, my father pulled out his gun and shot some blanks into the air. To his surprise, Samoné began screaming in a convincing imitation of a woman's voice: "Please, don't kill me! Don't kill me, please, I beg you!"

My uncle then took up the cue, shouting: "Oh yes, I will! Prepare to die!"

He then signaled to my father to shoot again. Meanwhile, my father was completely dismayed. This was not at all what he had had in mind; but he followed my uncle's suggestion and shot a few more blanks, which were accompanied by Samoné's piercing scream.

Then the three hurriedly returned to the house, my uncle and Samoné patting each other on the back and barely restraining their laughter, my father quite angry at both of them.

"You two are a pair of clowns," he scolded them when they arrived back at the courtyard. Then he stalked off to bed, leaving the other two men to rejoice in their prank.

It was well past midnight when we heard insistent knocks at our door. Someone was pounding the hand-shaped brass knocker with all his might. The lights came on, and my father opened the door, with all of us looking on, half-asleep in our pajamas and nightgowns.

A group of men had gathered outside, carrying flashlights and torches. Some were armed with revolvers, others with machetes.

"Didn't you hear anything?" one of them asked.

"A woman has been killed. You must have heard the shots!"

"Were those shots?" My father feigned surprise.

"We thought it was thunder," volunteered my mother.

"We must go find the body," insisted one of the men. "Will you come with us?" His words sounded more like a threat than an invitation.

My father and uncle rushed to get dressed and accompany the men. They did not want to find out how the armed men might react if they learned that what they had heard was only a prank.

The men searched the fields throughout the night, and for several days afterward. They crisscrossed the *marabú* fields, cutting new trails with their machetes. When at last they decided that the woman's body would not be found, a new legend was born.

A few months after all this took place, we moved from the big house to the city. We lived in the city for several years, until my father decided to open a road in the fields behind where the big house still stood and build a smaller house next to the river. When he tried to hire some people to clear the land, none of the locals were willing to do it. "It's a holy place," they said. "That land is sacred."

My father finally gave up trying to convince them, and instead brought in workers from the other side of town. Most of the land had already been cleared when the surprised workers found, in the very center of the *marabú* fields, mounds of objects commonly used as offerings: red ribbons, jars filled with American pennies, remains of sacrificial roosters. . . . Always respectful of other people's beliefs, my father asked the workers to leave that area untouched, although he well knew the origin of the "sacredness" of the place.

More than twenty years later, I had the opportunity to visit my homeland again, and I journeyed to this site of my childhood. The fields behind the house had changed greatly in those twenty years. They had been parceled into lots, and houses had been built. No sign remained of the *marabú* thickets.

I went to visit the family of our former caretakers. They had come to work for us from another region after the small house had been built, and knew nothing of the old prank.

Emilio, the father, welcomed me into his home. There in the living room stood a large altar. Flowers, candles, offerings of fruit, and statues of many different saints formed a colorful pyramid.

"Did you know that this is holy land, my child?" Emilio asked, disregarding the fact that my hair was already turning

gray. "You see, many years ago, a saintly woman lived in this area. She was killed when she refused to accept a man's advances. Since her body was holy, it disappeared and was never found. From that time on, her memory has been revered. . . ."

Nodding, I said nothing. I took his faith in this legend as a tribute to the sacredness of all women, and to the memory that we owe to the countless human beings who have indeed been victimized. Although I had a different take on this particular story, the validity of his faith was not for me to question.

I then followed Emilio to the backyard, where he proudly showed me his fruit trees: mangoes, *guayabos, chirimoyas, anones.*

"But Emilio," I asked, amazed, "wasn't all this an old stretch of dry riverbed? And wasn't there a steep ravine right behind your house?"

"I filled it in myself," Emilio said proudly. "For years, I wouldn't let myself go to bed without first bringing a few buckets of earth to empty into the gully." My eyes wandered slowly over the trees that he had planted in the old dry river bed, the former gully that he had filled in one bucket at a time with incredible patience. It then dawned on me that this land, painstakingly built up bit by bit, was indeed sacred, blessed by the true miracle of human faith and perseverance.

Chapter 7
Canelo

My mother and me

THE RAIN HAD barely stopped. I was ready to ask my mother for permission to go out and play when I saw the dog, a thinner dog than I'd ever seen before. His ribs seemed about to break through his skin. He had lost whole patches of hair and he looked as if he had just been rolling in the ashes of a campfire. But the saddest thing was to see him drag his hind leg, which hung black and lifeless as a piece of burned wood.

"*¡Papá, ayúdalo!* Help him!" I cried as I went looking for my father. "Please, help him get well again."

My mother, my aunts, and my uncle all rushed out to see why I was crying.

"Don't get close!" someone warned. "That dog is sick!"

"Poor animal! The only kind thing to do is to put him out of his misery."

"Yes. Let's put an end to his suffering," agreed another.

But I kept crying: "*¡Ayúdalo, Papá!* Please, help him." And my father, giving my hand a tight squeeze for reassurance, promised: "We'll help him get well."

Healing the dog was not a simple matter. My father brought some rope and tied it around his neck. The dog let himself be led by the rope, perhaps calmed by my father's soothing voice, or maybe just too exhausted to be able to protest.

My father tied him to the thick trunk of a *caimito* tree, behind the old coach house that stood halfway down the lane bordered by the flame trees. He covered the dog's body with a mixture of oil and sulfur. The small dog trembled but remained silent. The flies flew away, and now his broken leg was not black but gray and red instead.

"He has gangrene," said my father with a serious note in his voice. "He'll live only if I amputate his leg."

My mother brought cotton, rags, gauze, and a dark bottle. The rags soaked in chloroform put the dog to sleep. My father cut off the gangrenous leg with great precision, as if he were a surgeon instead of a surveyor, and carefully bandaged the stub.

"Now it's all a matter of whether he tears the bandage apart, or whether he allows the wound to heal," he said as he went off to disinfect his hands.

Never had there been a more cooperative patient. The small dog did not even attempt to touch the bandage.

In fact, he hardly moved at all, barely changing his position under the tree, and moving only as much as he needed to in order to remain in the shade. He only perked up when my father placed a half gourd filled with food scraps from the table in front of him.

I was forbidden to go too near the dog. Filled with both compassion and fear, I watched him from a distance. I would bring my doll over to visit him and stay nearby, playing the

solitary games of an only child, yet keeping the boundaries my
father had set.

As the dog lay on the *caimito* leaves, he would watch me
skip rope, or hop on one foot along the silhouette of a snail I
had traced with a stick in the soft earth. Little by little, his fur
grew back in the bald patches. And soon his ribs were not so
visible anymore. When my father finally took off the bandages,
I was happy to see that his stump had healed.

By then, we had begun calling him Canelo. And everyone
took it for granted that he would stay with us.

Once he was no longer confined by the rope, Canelo would
follow me, yet he always kept his distance. He would keep me
company, but never come close, just as I had kept him company from a distance while he was healing.

But with my father—what a different story! Every day, as
soon as my father got off the bus at the stop across the road,
Canelo would come running at full speed, moving more swiftly
on his three legs than if he'd had six. And all the while, he'd be
wagging his tail with as much energy and enthusiasm as a *bongó*
player drumming a *rumba*.

Chapter 8

The Rag Dolls

From left to right: my great-grandmother Mina; my grandmother Lola; my aunt Virginia; my cousin Virginita

Genoveva, my great-grandmother's sister

My GREAT-GRANDMOTHER, *mi bisabuela* Mina, was tiny, as time not only wrinkled but also shrunk her. She was not very much taller than the jasmine and the rose bushes she tended in her garden in the little house next to ours. Like the raisins she sprinkled generously in our *arroz con leche,* the rice pudding she made that smelled of cinnamon and cloves, her wrinkled form was filled with sweetness.

When *mi bisabuela* was not in the kitchen or in the garden, she would often sit in a rocking chair and sew. In her hands, scraps of cloth became multicolored quilts of various sizes. The large ones were wedding gifts for her many granddaughters; the small ones, greeting gifts for new great-grandchildren.

Yet the best pieces of cloth Mina saved for her rag dolls. As the light left her eyes and they became covered with an opaque glaze, she spent less and less time in the kitchen and the garden. Unable to see, she could not stitch together scraps and patches, so she stopped making quilts and took to crochet. But her blindness did not prevent her from making dolls. Her fingers, which had created dolls for so long, were able to give shape to the dolls' heads, to braid wool for their hair, to form their bodies and limbs.

Because she could not see the colors, I would help separate the greens and blues and reds that would become long skirts and bright head scarves. She would ask me: "This soft velvety piece, is it black? Can you find me a nice dark brown? A creamy chocolate? A toasted almond? A bright cinnamon?" And so the dolls would receive faces that resembled those of the neighborhood children.

Once a week, her sister Genoveva came to visit from the other end of town, and on each doll she would embroider the dark round eyes, the lips, and the two dots for a nose.

The dolls sat on the windowsill, four, five, six at a time. Little girls—some carrying cans full of water that their mothers needed to do the laundry, others loaded down with a bag of coal for cooking, and pulling a reluctant little brother or sister by the hand—would take a quick look to see whether the dolls had changed from the previous week. Or maybe, late in the afternoon, free of chores, skipping on one foot, jumping with a frayed rope, they would glance in the direction of the window and smile.

Whenever birthdays approached, mothers came knocking at Mina's door, holding in their hands an old handkerchief with coins tied up in a corner. "How much for the one with the red skirt?" they would ask. "And for the pretty one with the braids?"

Sunken in her rocking chair, my great-grandmother,

sightless, knew. She knew when to say twenty-five cents, thirty, forty, to honor the woman's pride, to allow her the joy of giving. She also knew when to say, "I'd like so much for Marisa to have it. Seven she'll be, won't she?" and hand it to the mother saying, "Just save me some scraps, I'll make another one. . . ."

At other times, a young mother, weathered down by long hours of laundering and boiling clothes under the sun, of cooking in makeshift stoves made of old lard cans, would come to my grandmother's house, saying only, "I've brought you a few oranges, or mangoes, or some watercress . . ." and my great-grandmother would close her sightless eyes a moment, concentrating, before saying, "Oh yes, Manuelita will be five very soon now, won't she? Isn't it time she had her own doll? Do you see any she would like?" The mother's hand would go up to her face, to cover a bashful smile. And the doll would leave its place on the front window, wrapped in the old newspaper that had previously held the golden, red, green offerings.

Chapter 9

Mathematics

Two photos of me when I was young

My little sister, Flor, and me

My GREAT-GRANDMOTHER MINA never went to school. She never learned to read or write. And she never studied the multiplication tables.

When she heard me trying to memorize three times three equals nine, three times four equals twelve, she'd say, "My sweet God, child, what are you doing? Becoming like my Cotita?" Cotita was her green parrot, which perched on a metal ring in her kitchen.

As she grew older and more frail, Mina spent most of her days in bed. She had borne five daughters and a son before my great-grandfather had abandoned her. As fate would have it, their lives turned out very differently. Two children became landowners, like their father before them; two lived in extreme poverty; while the other two were comfortable, if not rich. And as each of those six children had his or her own children, the diversity in their lives became even greater. But they all had in common their love for the little weathered woman who lived simply in the poor, tiny house next to ours, with her seventh child, a son born much later to a different father.

All of her children, rich and poor, dropped by to see her often. And because there were so many grandchildren and great-grandchildren, someone would come by to visit every day. Seldom did they come with empty hands; and the gifts they brought reflected the means of the giver.

Mi bisabuela Mina greeted each one of her visitors as if he or she were the most important person in the world to her, which at that moment was undoubtedly true. She shared jokes, always remembering who had told her the joke in the first place. And she'd tell the visitor the latest news about everyone in the family. So although the children had drifted apart, following their own paths, she remained a constant link between them. But mainly she listened, somehow drawing from each visitor that which was truly important to hear.

Mina received the presents that were offered to her with great joy and a mischievous smile. She was as pleased by a bunch of wildflowers or an orange as she was by a pair of slippers, a shawl, or a set of towels. She would then point to her closet. "On the second shelf," she would say, "to the left," with precise instructions, as if her blind eyes could still see, "there's a can of peaches." Or she'd explain, "In the top drawer, to the right, there's a box of handkerchiefs."

And in this way, the poor granddaughter who came in with a few oranges would go home with a new pair of socks. The tired daughter who brought a jar of homemade guava jelly would leave with a scarf or with an envelope that would help meet the rent payment. And the rich son would receive the gift of an orange. All were given with the greatest simplicity, and with utmost joy.

My great-grandmother Mina, who never went to school, who could not read and never learned the multiplication tables, but who remembered the birth date and the exact age of seven children, thirty-four grandchildren, seventy-five great-grandchildren, and a few great-great-grandchildren, knew a different kind of mathematics from the heartless tables I learned by rote. She knew how to add and subtract, how to accept and to give and to share so that the balance was always one of love.

Chapter 10

The Ice-Cream Man

An ice-cream man sells his wares in Camagüey, present day

AT HOME THEY kept reminding us of the war, World War II, especially during meals. "Before the war," my parents and aunts would say, "there was plenty of butter. Now we have to make our own."

My mother would save the cream that gathered at the top whenever she boiled fresh milk, adding a little more each day to the jar stored in the refrigerator. Once a week, she let me beat the cream into butter with a wooden spoon in a big bowl. When my arms began to ache, she would wash the butter with ice water in order to separate the curd from the whey. The butter we made was white, not yellow, but to me it tasted fresh and wonderful. I didn't know or miss any other kind, nor did I believe, no matter what they said, that any butter could taste better than what we had.

The adults also complained of the lack of white sugar, "so abundant," they would say, "before the war." Yet I loved the coarse brown sugar we had. Many days, for an afternoon snack, my mother would pinch a hole in a roll and fill it with brown sugar. I thought it was quite a treat.

The war was far away and distant, an empty word for a girl who loved homemade butter and brown sugar and enjoyed collecting the aluminum wrappers from the occasional choco-late Kiss my aunts would bring home from the movies.

Another complaint my mother and aunts had—the lack of cosmetics and nylon stockings—meant even less to me. And as for saving the slivers of soap—the fragrant soaps we used in the bathroom, the coarse yellow soap used for washing clothes and dishes—I found it an interesting project. The remnants were melted together in a tin can, yielding a multicolored, multipurpose bar in the shape of the can. To this day, I remem-ber the smell of boiling soap, and I collect tiny bars from hotels I visit in memory of those early years.

Although the shortages of things like butter and soap dur-ing the war didn't bother me, war showed its ugly face one day in school. I was attending St. Paul's Episcopal School, one of the two American schools that existed in my town at the time. We wore a uniform of a sickly mustard color and were teased mercilessly by the children of the two nearby Catholic schools. But our parents were pleased that we had the opportunity to learn English and to be educated bilingually, so there we went. For days our teachers had promised that they were going to give us some free comic books to take home. We couldn't wait to receive them. Comics, which usually appeared only in the Sunday paper, were a treat that we waited for all week long. A whole book of comics for our very own seemed so special that it was hard to imagine. But when at last the long-awaited day came, what we were given was not very funny at all.

Some of my friends were hoping for comic books of Blondie, others wanted Donald Duck or Mickey Mouse, some of the boys looked forward to Tarzan or cowboy stories. Secretly, I was hoping for Prince Valiant. But instead of the type of comic book characters that we knew so well from the newspaper, these comic books depicted the fighting in the Pacific Ocean. In them the Japanese were shown as short, monsterlike creatures, painted a bright yellow, with unnaturally slanted eyes that made their faces look like fierce masks.

I had only met one Japanese person in my life. He was indeed small, even to my child's eyes, but he was not yellow, and his almond-shaped eyes looked bright and calm. He pushed an old ice-cream cart throughout the city, visiting a different neighborhood each day, as if to give everyone a chance to taste the delicious flavors of his ice cream: pineapple, coconut, chirimoya, and more.

My parents did not usually allow me to eat things sold by the vendors on the streets. "It's made with unclean water. You can get terrible diseases from unclean water," my father would say, in a tone that allowed no arguments. But they always let me buy ice cream from the Japanese man. "He boils the water," my mother assured us. "He makes sure that his food is clean."

The Japanese man's ice cream was different from any other ice cream sold in stores or restaurants. It was lighter, and instead of the heavy, sugary taste so prevalent in Cuban desserts, it possessed only the natural sweetness of the fruits

themselves. To me it seemed as if the essence of the fruit had magically become light and cold, without ceasing to be fruit.

The Japanese man served his ice cream differently, too. For him, it was almost an art. Instead of filling a little paper cup, or plopping a scoop of ice cream on a cone, he would spread it on a thick waffle with a spatula, gently and evenly. Then he would cover it with another waffle, creating a thick ice-cream sandwich that sold for a nickel.

For those who could not afford to spend a whole nickel on ice cream, he had little waffle boats. The larger ones sold for two cents apiece, while the smaller ones were a penny. In these he packed the ice cream carefully too, filling the delicate boat to the brim, and then adding an extra dollop on top.

But often even a penny was too much for many of the children in my town. For every child who was able to purchase ice cream, there were two or three onlookers eyeing the meticulous process carefully, wishing that they too could taste the cool fresh coconut, banana, or guava.

The ice-cream man would take a quick glance around to make sure no adults were watching, that his next act of kindness would go unseen. And then he would lift the top of the wooden box in the front of the cart, where the waffles were kept, dig into a corner, and pull out some pieces of broken waffle. He would spread a dab of ice cream on each piece, and silently hand one to each of the hopeful children, with merely a hint of a soft smile on his face. Then he would close the lid and continue pushing the old cart along the streets.

He never yelled *"¡Helado! ¡Heladeeero!"* like the other raucous ice-cream vendors did. He did not ring a bell nor blow a whistle. Yet somehow we always knew when he was in the neighborhood.

After I looked through the comic books I had been given to take home, the comic books that showed the hideous yellow faces, I tore each one to pieces, page by page, feeling sadness and great shame. How could it be, I wondered, that people could hate one another so much that they would want to fight and kill each other? I wanted no one else to see the little yellow monsters, because in my short years I had already met a real Japanese person, and he had brought a fresh and fragrant kindness to the streets of my small town.

Chapter 11

Fiesta de San Juan

My great-grandfather, Federico Salvador Arias, with his family. Their car has been decorated for the Fiesta de San Juan

"*¡M*ONO VIEJO! *¡FRIJOLITO!*" "Old monkey! Little bean!" taunted a group of boys. They followed a man wearing a colorful costume made of a floral fabric, that covered him from head to toe save for openings for his eyes and mouth.

Hearing the boys' cries, the *mono viejo* turned around. Dozens of bells covered his outfit and filled the street with a jingling sound as he made threatening gestures toward the children with his thick tail. This long piece of heavy rope was also covered with floral fabric, and had larger, heavier bells sewn onto it.

The children screamed and scattered, each running in a different direction, seeking refuge on porches and among the narrow, crooked alleys. The *mono viejo* continued with his pranks and antics, jumping and somersaulting throughout the streets of the town, until another group of children gathered the courage to cry out: "*¡Mono viejo! ¡Frijolito!*"

It was the *Fiesta de San Juan,* or St. John's Feast, which lasted throughout the month of June. In Cuba, as in much of Spain and Latin America, each town celebrated with a feast on the day of the town's patron saint, according to the Catholic tradition. Camagüey's patron saint is San Juan, whose feast day

is June 24. But since June 29 is also a very special day—the
Feast of St. Peter and St. Paul—and it's only five days away, the
celebrations ran until that date.

Preparations for the carnival-like feast began early. By
the first week of June, the town's appearance had begun to
change. The old walls of brick and mortar blossomed as each
neighborhood competed to be the best decorated. Triumphal
arches appeared everywhere, garlanded with palm fronds and
flame tree branches in full bloom. In some neighborhoods,
young boys stretched a rope across the street to stop passing
cars and ask for donations to decorate their street. In other
areas of town, flame tree branches and palm fronds gave way
to paper flowers and brightly colored lights.

During the *Fiesta de San Juan*, all the social rules disappeared. In a town where everyone knew everyone else, where
social codes were rigid and strict, and where no action passed
unnoticed or unmentioned, everything was allowed during
this month of the year. Men could dress as women, and everyone could follow his or her fancy to be a pirate or a princess,
a courtly lady or a page, Superman or Tarzan, harlequin or
queen. It was common for pale-skinned people to choose to
wear black faces for Carnival, for once acknowledging their
hidden and denied African heritage.

Those who did not have a favorite fantasy and whose only
goal was to have fun became *mamarrachos*. To do so, all you
needed was to disguise all of your identifiable features. And

so hair disappeared behind a stocking, hands inside a pair of socks, faces behind masks or perhaps behind fake noses and makeup. Anything worked as long as no one, not even the *mamarracho's* own mother, could recognize him or her. Now, by changing their voices, the *mamarrachos* could appear at the homes of friends and neighbors, laugh and joke with every passerby, flirt with respectable matrons, and make fun of the solemn members of the Professional Society—those who could add the title "doctor" before their name and sit pompously at their exclusive club.

At night, parades of floats rode through the central streets of town, followed by horse-drawn carriages brought in by railroad from all over the island especially for the occasion. Flatbed trucks also joined the parade, carrying noisy groups of revelers who threw confetti and streamers at the people who filled the streets.

The parade became even livelier when the *comparsas* appeared. These groups of twenty, forty, or sixty men and women in matching costumes carried *farolas*—long, decorated poles with lanterns on top. As the *comparsas* went by, moving as one in intricate dances, the people on the sidewalks, in doorways, and at windows all danced to their rhythm too, letting themselves be carried away by the music. Moving their shoulders, waists, and hips to the rhythm, they would sing along:

Mírala, ¡qué linda viene!

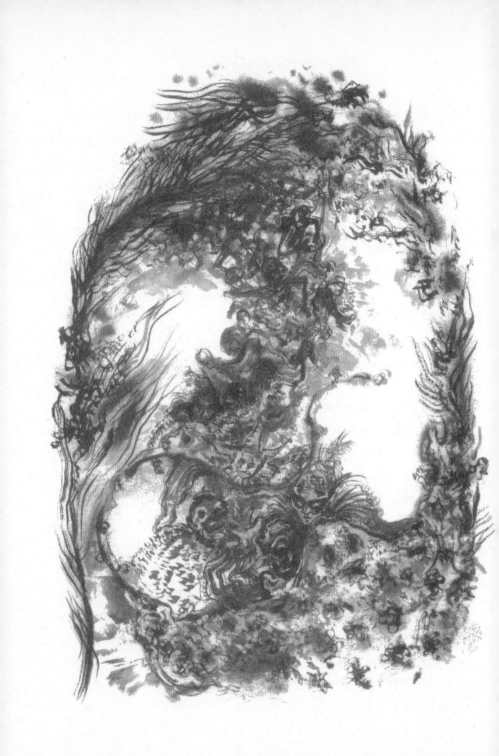

Mírala, ¡qué linda va!
La comparsa "Maravillas"
que se va y no vuelve más.

Look, she is a beauty as she comes!
Look, she is a beauty as she goes!
The *comparsa* "Many wonders"
leaves and will return no more.

More floats, carriages, and decorated trucks full of costumed people would come, and then another *comparsa*. Arms in ruffled sleeves held the tall *farolas* high, and everyone, those taking part in the *comparsa* and those looking on from the sidewalk, men and women, parents and children, grandparents and grandchildren, would sing:

Al Carnaval de Oriente no voy.
En Camagüey, ¡se goza mejor!

I won't go off to Oriente for Carnival.
In Camagüey, we have it all!

At long last the parade would near its end . . . but what an end it was! It was time now for *congas*. Rolling their bodies to the rhythm of the *bongós* and the *tumbadoras,* the *congas* appeared: large groups of people dancing together, yet not in

choreographed lines like the *comparsas*. Their rhythmic music
had a melody that could be sung:

Uno, dos y tres,
que paso más chévere,
que paso más chévere,
el de mi conga es.

Al tambor mayor delante
nadie lo puede igualar
con el ritmo fascinante
de mi Cuba tropical.

One, two, three,
what a joyful step,
what a joyful step,
of my conga roll.

The head drum that leads the drumming
has no equal to its beat
for you see it has the rhythm
of my Cuban island heat.

The first *congas* to arrive might resemble the preceding,
more orderly *comparsas*. But very soon, all resemblance disappeared. What coursed through the street was clearly the energy

of the people. Perhaps there still remained a *bongó,* or a *tumbadora* drum, but now what predominated was the persistent rhythm, hypnotic and alluring, of steel against steel—old car wheels that had been turned into drums, struck with an iron rod.

As the majestic river of people flooded the streets with its powerful rhythms, everything that had appeared before became mere prelude. The courtly ladies with pow-dered wigs, the queen and her attendants, the harlequins, the false strength of make-believe Supermen, all vanished as the streets surrendered to the memory of jungles and of rivers, of ancestral rites of hunting, planting, and mat-ing, rites once forgotten and still very much alive in the blood that now pounded to the accelerated beat of the *congas.* Blood that will never again be mine alone, but instead ours, blood that courses not only through my veins, but through all of us as one, reconnecting us with our roots—these powerful, vigorous African roots, once shamefully enslaved, now free, redeemed by the power of this driving rhythm, free and calling to be honored, now and for all time.

Epilogue

Under the flame trees, on Aunt Mireya's shoulders

As a child of the countryside and the open air, our move to town was difficult for me. Like a plant transplanted into too small a pot, lacking sunshine and rain, I withered. But as the *congas* rolled along the streets of our town, I—half-hidden behind the door, fearful of the strength of the drums—woke up to the echo of their rhythm in my blood.

As I watched the crowd, growing from several dozen people to several hundred, beating their drums, whether of hide or steel, I realized that my own roots extended very far indeed.

Some of them came from Spain, when my grandfather Modesto hid as a stowaway on a ship or when my grandfather Medardo left because he couldn't marry the cousin he loved. But my roots also went deep into the Cuban soil, to the *siboneyes* whose indomitable spirit remains in the proud royal palms and whose language echoes in the name of my town, Camagüey, and in the name of our river, the Tínima. And my roots also reached far back to Africa, to the land whose rhythms were voiced by the drums, the land where the majestic *ceibas* send their sacred branches up toward the sky.

While these roots nourished me, the tree trunks that grew

all around invited me to climb high, to watch the world from the vantage point of their branches.

My father once built me a tree house up in the branches of an *algarrobo,* a magnificent tree growing by the river. From that hideout, if I stayed as quiet as the herons, I could watch the *jicoteas* come out to bask in the sun, the frogs hopping and leaping after flies, and the *biajacas y guajacones* glistening under the water. The whole world of the river was right there before me.

From the security of my home, I could also observe the world around me: the street vendors, the beggars, the people on the street—each one with their own life, their own story to tell.

As I write these lines, fall is arriving to the mountains of northern California where I now live. As the leaves turn bright yellow and deep red, I absorb their powerful colors. Occasionally one leaf will catch my attention, perhaps because its shape is so perfect, or its color so intense—and so I pick it up, and bring it inside. And it is as though with that one leaf, I have somehow brought the whole forest to my desk.

And so it is with these stories. There are still many more of them, hanging on the branches of the trees of my childhood. I have picked a few, hoping to give you a taste of those bygone days sweetened by mangoes and guavas, perfumed by the fragrance of orange blossoms, brightened by the fiery branches of the flame trees in bloom.

Days at
La Quinta
Simoni

with illustrations by Edel Rodriguez

To all the members of the Lafuente-Salvador family, whose roots reach back to La Quinta Simoni, in hopes that they will always value their heritage of kindness, generosity, courage, creativity, and responsibility

Introduction

La Quinta Simoni with, left to right, me, my cousin Virginita, my aunt Virginia, and my grandmother Lola

AT LA QUINTA Simoni, the weathered old house where I was born and where I lived for much of my childhood, the magic began early in the morning when my grandmother would wake me up for our daily visit to the cows. In Cuba, only prized cows in large *haciendas* lived in barns; our handful of cows lived outdoors, grazing on grass all year round. When our farmhand milked the cows under a tree, my grandmother would hand him a large glass and he would direct a squirt of milk straight into it. She always let me drink first, and as I raised the glass, holding it with both hands, the foam on top would tickle my nose.

Later in the day, the magic continued. I was allowed to roam our fields freely, and I would spend long stretches of time by the river, observing the fish: the small *guajacones* who skimmed the surface, eating mosquito larvae; the swift *biajacas* swimming deep in the water; the brown *renacuajos,* tadpoles at different stages of turning into frogs. The large green tadpoles with yellow bellies would turn into *ranas toro,* the bull frogs we heard at night—since these were not easy to spot, seeing one was a rare treat. This was also true of *jicoteas,* river turtles whose hearing was very sharp;

no matter how quietly I approached, all I could see were the ripples they left behind, because they would jump off their rocks and into the water before I even reached the river.

There was also the large fallen tree that lay on the ground close to the river: a resting giant with a number of branches that grew straight up from its side. If I had known then what a harp looked like, I would have said it resembled one. Instead, for me, the fallen tree was a many-masted sailing ship on a daring voyage, and I read many tales of adventure while nestled there.

Our own patio was filled with a multitude of wonders: the fragrance of orange blossoms, particularly after it rained; the surprise of finding lizards' eggs under the ferns; the excitement of watching my grandmother's many hens gather around us as we fed them ground corn or fresh *canutillo* leaves harvested from the river banks.

And there was a powerful magic in my grandmother's stories. When recounting the heroic deeds of Cuban patriots during the struggle for independence, she would always remind me that the brave and wise Ignacio Agramonte had wooed his sweetheart, Amalia Simoni, right here in this garden. My grandmother's stories about the ancient Greek gods made them feel so real that I imagined them around every corner. And her animal stories changed with each delightful retelling, weaving in details of whatever was happening around us.

There was truly wonder everywhere. In kites flying on windy days, in paper boats sailing after the rains, and in the simple games we played to tunes that had been sung for hundreds of years.

Capturing the magic of these simple days at La Quinta Simoni and passing it on to you: that is what the following stories are all about.

Chapter 1
Street Vendors' Voices

The knife sharpener's wheel

A man pedals through the streets of Camagüey, present day

THE FIRST VENDOR to call out his wares each morning was the *panadero,* the baker.

> *Pan . . . panadero. . . calentito . . .*
> *pan de leche . . . pan de huevo . . . calentito . . .*

> Fresh-baked bread . . . the baker's here . . . warm bread . . .
> milk bread . . . egg bread . . . still warm from the oven . . .

Housewives and maids rushed out at his call. After choosing that morning's fragrant bread, they brought in their milk bottles; while everyone else was sleeping, the milkman had already made his rounds, delivering milk in his bright yellow horse-drawn cart.

The baker's bread came to us right from the oven. Sometimes we dipped it in *café con leche*—warm milk with a few drops of very strong coffee—or we covered it with butter and savored each small bite.

The *panadero* was a large man whose bald head shone under the morning sun. His white cart was pulled by a white horse. Most of the horses that pulled carts through the city were skinny and hungry-looking. In contrast, the baker's horse was robust and shiny, like his owner.

Every morning, I waited eagerly for the baker's cart. I loved the warm bread and the *panadero*'s warm smile. He would pick me up with his strong arms and set me on the seat next to him. Surrounded by the delicious scent of bread, I felt like Cinderella in her coach during the very brief ride to my great-grandmother's house next door. In those early mornings, when I was three years old, there was not the slightest doubt in my mind that when I grew up, I would marry the baker.

The vendors' calls continued throughout the day. The *viandero* sold the tasty roots that were a daily part of Cuban meals. As he tugged at the muzzle of his mule, loaded with two heavy baskets, he called:

> *Malanga blanquita . . . yuca tierna . . .*
> *boniatos dulces . . .*

> White taro root . . . tender cassava . . .
> delicious sweet potatoes . . .

The *viandero* smiled as he pulled the *viandas* out from the depths of his immense straw baskets.

"Look, *caserita*, look at this pumpkin! The *yucas* are really tender. Don't you want some *ñame*? The potatoes are very good. For *papas fritas*, for *puré de papas* . . . fry them, mash them . . . and what about the corn? You will not find such tender corn anywhere else, *caserita*. . . ."

Most sellers called their female customers *"casera"* or "housewife." Yet *"caserita"* was a term of endearment, and it made my mother smile.

The *viandero* passed the fruits of the earth into Mamá's arms. When she could not hold any more, he placed a large piece of pumpkin, bright orange with a thick green crust, into my hands. "A little bit of *calabaza, niña,* to make the soup more tasty," he said.

The tall, thin man who sold fresh vegetables did not cry out to announce his presence. Silently, he lowered the two flat baskets that hung from his shoulders on the ends of a long pole and set them on the sidewalk. He greeted my mother with great dignity, as though presenting precious jewels instead of tender lettuce, pungent radishes, and bright peppers. It felt magical, as though Aladdin's lamp had transported a flowering garden to our door.

Mamá always made her selection carefully, trying not to destroy the artistic display of greens and vegetables—the long and tender green beans, small bunches of watercress, a perfectly round cabbage. While she made her choices, she would try to engage the vendor in conversation: "And in China . . . ," she would ask, "do radishes as good as these grow in China?"

Although he was normally serious, the man would smile silently and so broadly that his eyes would disappear into his face.

One morning, almost before saying *"Buenos días,"* his usual reserved demeanor disappeared as he said to my mother:

"This, *señora*, this is what grows in China . . . twelve years without seeing him, until I was able to make the money." And he pushed forward, proudly, a boy so shy that he could not raise his eyes from the ground.

"Look, *señora*, my son . . . twelve years without seeing him. . . ." And he laughed joyfully, allowing us to admire his truest treasure: the treasure for whom he had cultivated tomatoes and lettuce, watercress and radishes, carrots and eggplants, for such a long time and with so much care.

Sometimes the call we heard was musical, like the whistle of the knife sharpener who walked through the streets of the city, pushing a simple wheelbarrow that carried his whetstone. Whenever someone needed him to sharpen a kitchen knife, a pair of scissors, or a machete, he would set down the wheelbarrow and step on his pedal to make the round stone turn.

The sharpener's whistle reminded my mother of a tango, and she would always burst out singing:

Afilador,

no abandones tu pedal;
dale que dale a la rueda
que con tantas vueltas
ya la encontrarás . . .

Wheel grinder,
Don't ease up on your pedal.
Make the wheel go round and round.
In one of those many turns
You will finally find her . . .

Afternoons belonged to the *dulceros,* the sellers of sweets. There was one such seller who stretched out the name of a favorite coconut treat while he walked, calling out:

Coquito acaramelao-o-o-o . . .

On one shoulder he carried a box filled with sweets, and on the other, a folded wooden stand.

Through the glass sides of the box, we could see the small *dulce de leche* squares and the brown balls of *dulce de coco.* While I liked them all, I had no trouble choosing the *coquitos acaramelados.* Their light candy shells contained white balls of grated coconut, floating in syrup. They were unquestionably my favorite sweet treat.

～

Another call that made me rush outside was:

Barquillos, barquilleeero . . .

Rolled wafers, the wafer vender is here . . .

The *barquillero* did not sell the crisp rolled wafers directly; instead, he carried them inside a tin canister with a roulette wheel on its lid. For the price of a coin, we could spin the pointer. The number where the pointer landed showed how many wafers we would receive: from 1 or 2, the most frequent numbers, to 20. I kept hoping that someday the pointer would land on that 20.

Cuban ingenuity manifested itself in many ways. The *manisero,* seller of peanuts or *maníes,* had constructed a portable oven out of an empty square can by adding a handle and a double bottom. In the second bottom sat a layer of burning coals, used to warm the brown paper cones full of peanuts.

The peanut seller's characteristic call of *"Maní, maniseroooo . . ."* inspired one of the most popular Cuban songs of all time. For this reason, whenever his call was heard, someone would inevitably begin to sing:

Maní, manisero se va . . .
cuando la calle sola está,

casera de mi corazón,
el manisero entona su pregón
y si la niña escucha su canción
llamará desde el balcón.
Maní, manisero se va.
Caserita no te acuestes a dormir
sin comerte un cucurucho de maní.

Peanuts, the peanut vendor is leaving . . .
when the street is empty,
casera of my heart,
the peanut vendor sends forth his call
and if a girl hears his song
she will call down from her balcony.
Peanuts, the peanuts vendor is leaving.
Caserita, don't go to sleep
until you have eaten your peanuts.

Like the *manisero,* the *tamalero* used a can turned into a portable
oven to transport his goods.

Tamales . . .
Con picante y sin picante . . .

Tamales . . .
Spicy or plain . . .

The corn *masa* contained small pieces of pork, and if one asked for a *tamal con picante,* it would also contain hot red specks of chili. The dry corn husks were perfect wrappings for the *tamales.*

While seldom part of a regular Cuban meal, *tamales* were a special treat often enjoyed in the early evening. My aunt and uncle frequently answered the *tamalero's* call, and I loved it when they saved me a little piece.

But of all the vendors, the one whose call I awaited most eagerly was the *empanadillero,* the seller of *empanadillas:*

De guayaba y carne . . .

Guava-filled or meat-filled . . .

How I loved *empanadillas!* They could be savory, with a thick and substantial cornmeal crust, filled with tasty ground meat and seasoned with raisins and olives. Or they could be sweet and light, made of wheat flour and filled with *conserva de guayaba.* When the *empanadillas* were fried, the guava preserves inside would melt. If the *empanadillas* were still warm, the melted guava would run into our mouths as we bit into them.

One evening, my parents finally let me purchase the

empanadillas myself. I approached the *empanadillero* with a five-cent coin in hand, just as my father usually did.

"How much are they?" I asked, trying to sound grown up in my four-year-old voice.

"Two for five cents," the man answered politely.

I thought for a moment. If two identical *empanadillas* were worth five cents combined, that meant he was charging three cents for one and only two for the other. So I said, very sure of myself:

"Give me two. But make sure they are the ones for which you only charge two cents."

The man laughed, surprised by my reasoning. He wrapped two *empanadillas* and gave me back one cent.

I walked into the house beaming with pride. Not only did I have the two *empanadillas* we bought every night, but this time I had a cent all my own. With that one cent, I could buy a small package that contained a cookie and a picture card to paste into my *Gulliver's Travels* album.

But to my great surprise, my father did not praise how I had used my math skills. "God did not make you smart so you could take advantage of others," Papá said, his voice sounding more stern than usual. "Now, who do you think needs that one cent more—you, who wants to buy a cookie, or the *empanadillero* who spends his life selling *empanadillas,* two for five cents?" He did not wait for an answer, but left me alone to ponder his question.

The next day under the *carolinas* tree, my favorite spot in the garden, I studied the one-cent coin. On one side, it showed the lone star of the Cuban flag; on the other, the national seal.

The kiosk where they sold cookies was just at the end of the garden. My parents did not encourage my desire to complete my card collection; they only gave me one cent a week to buy a cookie, so my album was filling very slowly. Now I had the opportunity to get an extra card. What card would I get if I bought a cookie . . . a number four, which would allow me to complete the first page of my album? Or maybe the card that showed Gulliver tied up by the tiny men of Lilliput?

That afternoon, I asked for permission to purchase the *empanadillas* again. My father, without saying a word, handed me a five-cent coin.

I ran to the porch as soon as I heard the call:

Empanadiii . . . llas

Then I asked the *empanadillero:* "One meat and one *guayaba, por favor.*"

When he gave them to me, with the same gentle smile he had shown me the previous evening, I gave him the five-cent coin plus the cent I had kept all day in my pocket. "These ones," I said, "are three cents each."

And while the man looked down in surprise at the six cents in his palm, I went back inside, with warm *empanadillas* in my hand and a warm new feeling in my heart.

Chapter 2

Paper Boats

After a coconut
harvest, in 1938

My father, my
mother, and me

IN CUBA, ONE sunny day follows another—until the rainy season begins. Rain showers punctuate daily life. Farmers wait for the rain to water their fields, and city dwellers wait for it to wash down the streets and mitigate the heat.

As children, we eagerly awaited the rain, as it marked the beginning of the mango season. "Mangoes only ripen after the first rains," our mothers explained. "Mangoes gathered before the rains begin will give you a bellyache," cautioned our grandmothers.

For this reason, the spring rains were received with great joy. Now we could eat the delightful fruit: the perfectly golden *mangos de mamey,* the large red *mangos del Caney,* and the stringy *mangos de hilacha,* which we did not eat, but rather slurped. *Mangos de hilacha* are not cut or peeled, but instead pounded softly and evenly until all the pulp turns to liquid; then one bites away a small piece of the peel and slowly savors the flavorful juice.

Yet the rainy season also meant having to stay indoors, unless it was just a gentle shower. Sometimes Mamá decided to join me to play outdoors in the light rain. Instead of going by myself to the quiet garden and its trees, we would run together into the courtyard. There, we would step around the flower beds to stand directly under the stream of water that poured down from the gutters. We called this *"bañarnos en el aguacero."* The strong downpour landed on our backs as we screamed, our mouths filling with water as our hearts filled with joy.

But whenever the rain was accompanied by thunder and lightning, it was not safe to play outside. Tropical storms could last all day, and the long hours inside the house—in those times before I learned to read—seemed to last forever.

Fortunately, my caring father had a special remedy for those days: He let me look inside his special drawer, which I called *la gavetita.*

La gavetita was one of the drawers in his large rolltop desk. The excitement began the moment I saw him roll back the cover to reveal the fascinating instruments he used in his work as a surveyor.

Papá would then take out the small drawer, *la gavetita,* and place it where I could look inside. He would always give the same instructions: "You can take anything you want, but only one thing. Think about it carefully, because once you choose, you will not be able to change your mind."

The drawer was full of the most unexpected things: shiny marbles, pencil stubs of all sizes and colors, erasers, clips, buckles, shells, safe scissors, coins from many countries, various kinds of keys, dice of different sizes, single dominoes, and puzzle pieces . . . all objects my father had found scattered around the house or had brought home from his frequent trips.

It took a long time to go through this treasure trove. How well I understood, then, Aladdin's marvel and Ali Baba's difficulties! On some occasions, my choice was easy—for example, when I had not been able to play jacks for several days because I had lost the rubber ball that now smiled up at me from the drawer. But most of the time, choosing was impossible. How could I choose between a seal with my grandfather's initials and a large blue marble; between a small gold key and a barrette for my doll; or between a magnifying glass and a prism that hid a permanent rainbow?

By the time I finally made my choice, the rain had usually stopped. Water would be running down the sides of the street, and my father would be waiting for me with an old newspaper in his hands.

Papá would fold the newspaper carefully, bringing the corners together to form a perfect square. Then, after folding it several times, he turned it into a boat with a central sail. Sometimes I asked him to fold it once more, to create two small canopies at the prow and stern.

Papá used several newspaper sheets for each boat so that they would be strong and make long journeys. As he finished each one, he placed it carefully in the running water.

Sitting on the low windowsill behind the carved wooden railings, I watched the boats sailing along under the clearing skies, carrying my childhood dreams and my father's love.

Chapter 3
Kites

My father and mother

My mother

IN THE CARIBBEAN, August and September are months that bring hurricanes and storms. The days when there was wind but no rain were kite-flying days.

As soon as we returned home from spending our summer vacation by the ocean, Papá would begin to talk about making me a kite. I was impatient to see the kites dancing in the sky, yet I knew that before that could happen, there would be another type of dance. This dance would take place around our very large dining room table, where more than a dozen people would gather daily for meals, with me the only child.

Papá would spread out all the materials needed to make the kite across this table: *güines,* thin reeds for the frame; *papel de China,* a smooth, translucent paper that came in bright colors; *goma arábiga,* resin pellets that looked like burned caramels; and Papá's *cuchillo de mango blanco,* the sharp knife with an ivory handle that was his preferred tool for most tasks.

Then the dance began. While Papá sliced and tied the reeds together to form the frame of the kite, Mamá boiled the gum arabic in water, making the glue that was used to stick the paper onto the frame. They worked together, seldom speaking but

often smiling, pleased with their tasks. Each seemed to antici-
pate what the other needed at any given moment.

The China paper was very thin and could easily wrinkle.
Papá cut it carefully with his sharp knife. While he stretched it
and held it tightly, my mother spread the glue that held the various pieces together and bound them to the reeds.

Papá loved to make multicolored kites: yellow, green, red,
and orange. Flying in the air, they looked like giant parrots or
macaws escaped from the jungle. Mamá, on the other hand,
preferred to make kites that were all one color and looked more
like butterflies.

In Camagüey, we called our kites *barriletes*. Years later, I
learned that in the vast Spanish-speaking world, kites are called
by many different names. One of these is *papagayos,* which
means "parrots;" this name would have been very appropriate
for Papá's kites. And the widely used *papalote,* derived from the
Nahuatlan word *papalotl* that means "butterfly," would have
been perfect for Mamá's.

The wind was still blowing. Papá and Mamá had worked for a
long while, dancing around the dining room table. The result of
their efforts was one of Papá's colorful kites, a true *papagayo*—
orange, yellow, red, and green—and one of Mamá's kites, a
charming blue butterfly.

For kites to fly easily, they need a long, light tail. Usually,
these tails were made with scraps of cloth. But Mamá dreamed

up special tails for these special kites: To my father's surprise, she unrolled two old typewriter ribbons and tied a number of tiny bows on each one.

We took the kites across the street to fly at Plaza de La Habana, the large empty lot across from La Quinta Simoni. The beautiful kites with their long, light tails took to the air immediately, and soon they were high in the sky.

While my parents held on to the kite strings, I scribbled a secret message to each kite on small pieces of paper. "*Por favor,* Papá, Mamá, send my letters up to the kites."

They each made a tiny tear on their paper and placed it on the string. Soon, the air was nudging my notes up the strings and toward the kites.

That windy afternoon, thanks to Papá's careful handicraft and Mamá's ingenuity, our kites flew higher than any others. Dipping and swerving in the sky, they resembled my parents around our old dining room table, each moving freely, yet both flowing in a shared dance.

Chapter 4

Circle Games

My parents, with my older
cousin Virginita and me,
after an exciting horseback
riding adventure

Left to right: tía Virginia, tía Mireya,
Mamá, tía Lolita

Tía Virginia and me

At LA QUINTA Simoni we lived together as a large family. My grandmother, whom I called *mi paraíso,* taught me to read and filled my early years with her amazing stories; my parents, aunts, and uncle were always kind and caring. My great-grandmother Mina lived in a little house next door. But aside from her, we had no other neighbors nearby: La Quinta Simoni stood by itself at the edge of town. I found friends among the trees and the wild creatures I observed along the river, yet I longed to take part in the games that children played in the books I read.

Seeing how frequently I played with the girl that lived in her armoire mirror, my mother intuited this longing and decided to create a game for me. She gave me a few pieces of scrap paper and had me cut some into squares. Then she showed me how to make envelopes. Finally, we dipped some used envelopes in water to loosen the stamps. Mamá gave me a large old purse to keep my materials in, and she named me the house postwoman.

Every day I made two rounds. In the morning, people gave me the letters they had written to other members of the family, and they "bought" fresh paper, envelopes, and stamps from me.

In the afternoon, I would excitedly visit each person's room to deliver the mail I had for them that day.

Remembering this now, it amazes me that so many adults were willing to play this game just to keep me occupied and happy. But as fun as it was, selling postal materials and delivering letters filled only a small portion of my day.

One late afternoon, with the sun low in the sky, my mother called her sisters to the wide porch. "Remember the games we use to play here?" Before long, all three of them were running around, tagging each other.

My aunt Lolita asked: "Remember *'La Marisola'*?" We held hands to make a circle around her, and sang that old nursery rhyme.

Then my mother began skipping on one foot, singing, *"Desde chiquitica me quedé, algo resentida de este pie . . ."* ("Since I was very young, I've been unhappy with this foot . . .") and we followed her, laughing. After we finished, we sang another and another.

For a few weeks, my mother and aunts joined me every afternoon on the porch. Sometimes we played an old game, forming two lines and singing, *"Ambos a dos, materile, rile, rile."* Or two of us would hold our arms high to make an arch, while the others would weave single file beneath it to the tune of *"Al ánimo."* Other times, they taught me various rhymes as I skipped rope.

Gradually, to our surprise, children began to appear and join us in the games. And so, eventually, my mother and aunts left us alone to play while they returned to their many chores.

The children and I did not know each other formally. All of them lived several blocks away; some closer to town, others in the very poor neighborhoods far away from town. We did not go to the same schools, and it took me a while to learn their names. Yet every afternoon they would arrive almost all at once, like sparrows in the park gathering around scattered seeds.

Our games usually started with my mother's nursery rhymes, then moved into livelier ones. Sometimes we would pair up, facing each other and holding hands tightly, then spinning round and round while stretching backward, going faster and faster as we chanted: *"Bate, bate, chocolate."* ("Whip, whip, the chocolate.") Or we would go around in a circle, skipping as high as we could and singing, *"Salta, Perico, salta."* ("Jump, Perico, jump.")

For a tag game we called *La candelita,* or "small fire," each of us picked a "safe space" that we called *esquinas*, or "corners." These spots could be the various columns along the porch, or the edges of the tall windows that went all the way from the ceiling to the floor. One of us got to be "it" and had to beg for fire by going up to someone and asking, *"¿Una candelita?"* ("Can you give me fire?") In response, that child would point to another corner and answer, *"Por allá fumea. . . ."* ("There is smoke over there. . . .")

While the one seeking fire went off in that direction, every-one else had to try and change corners. But if the person who was "it" was fast enough, he or she could take over one of the empty corners, leaving someone else the task of asking for fire.

Around seven o'clock the children would disperse. Some were picked up by their parents, while most walked home by themselves. Some wore clothes made out of nice fabrics, while many wore clothes made out of bleached flour sacks. Some went to private schools and others to public schools, and a few had probably never gone to school at all. And yet, for those few hours on our front porch each day, those unfair differences did not keep us apart.

The hands that held one another in our circle games were pale, tan, or dark brown. Many in our town would have denied our equality; yet on those joyful afternoons, we knew we were brothers and sisters.

Chapter 5

Circus Days

I was so proud of my long braids.

¡EL CIRCO! THE circus! The circus is here!" I hollered as I ran through the garden. I wanted everyone to know: the birds, the shrubs, the lizards . . . even the ants and the crickets. Once again, the circus had arrived: the tightrope walkers who had us holding our breath in suspense, the jugglers who created rainbows of balls in the air, the clowns who made us cry from laughing so hard, and the female acrobat they called the Rubber Girl.

The circus raised its tent in Plaza de La Habana. In spite of the name, this was not a plaza, just a large empty plot of land. And it was not in La Habana, Cuba's capital, but right there in my very own city of Camagüey, just across the street from La Quinta Simoni.

Plaza de La Habana was not used for much. A few horses and mules often grazed lazily nearby, and on windy days, the neighborhood children went there to fly their kites, as I loved doing with my parents. On certain occasions, usually near election time, candidates would stand on wooden platforms there to make loud speeches filled with promises: to pave the streets . . . to widen the Central Highway . . . to build new schools . . . to add beds to the hospital. Promises, sadly, which were rarely fulfilled.

But once a year when the circus arrived, Plaza de La Habana was truly transformed. In addition to the large circus tent, there was a Ferris wheel and a carousel. There were also flying chairs, but I was not allowed to go on that ride, since there were rumors that once someone had actually flown *out* of a chair instead of remaining in it.

And then there was the food. . . . *Fritas* vendors came with their carts, filling the air with the tempting smells of hot oil and flavorful meat. Ice-cream sellers brought a delicious variety of flavors: white and creamy coconut, refreshing pineapple, and sweet *mamey,* which left our lips stained a deep red. There were kiosks selling *piñita Pijuán,* a pineapple soft drink that we preferred to any other.

For those few days, Plaza de La Habana ceased to be a dusty plain filled with weeds and became a land of miracles and wonders.

Before pitching his tarp, the circus owner, a tall man with a bushy mustache, would come to speak with my father. Since Plaza de La Habana had no source of water, he wanted permission to take water from the spigot next to the old carriage road on our property, a path we called *los framboyanes,* as it was lined by ancient flame trees. My father always agreed, and later, the circus owner would send someone from the circus—a clown, a juggler, or even a trapeze artist—to offer us a roll of pink tickets by way of thanks.

Circus days were comparable only to Christmas. I woke

up early, before anyone else, to meet the day's surprises. Yet no matter how early it was, the magic had already begun.

On our large front porch I'd find the circus owner's daughter, her body arched into a circle, head and toes almost touching. This was the Rubber Girl, practicing her contortionist act. As soon as she saw me standing openmouthed at our door, she would somersault from one end of the porch to the other, running away on her hands much quicker than I could follow on my feet. She would complete her routine with a curtsy, just as she did under the tarp at the end of each circus performance. Then she would jump across the street, hardly touching the pavement, and disappear between the tents and kiosks.

I would stay out on the porch for the longest time, not moving, thinking of how wonderful her life must be. To travel from city to city, to listen to people's applause, to stay up late and then fall asleep to the happy music from the kiosks—and most of all, to ride on the carousel every day, an idea as unimaginable to me as riding *los camellos de los Reyes Magos,* the Wise Men's camels.

We had just finished lunch. Although everyone else was taking *siestas,* I was sitting on the porch and reading *Little Women* for the third time when the circus girl came to fetch water. While she waited for the pail to fill, she spoke to me for the first time.

"What are you reading?" she asked.

I showed her the book cover.

"Is it nice?"

I couldn't believe that, being older than I was, she had never read *Little Women*. But she didn't leave me much time for wondering because she kept asking questions. She wanted to know if I went to school, what grade I was in, what I was learning.

In response I tried to explain my dream to her, of how much I would love to belong to the world of the circus. But now it was she who looked at me in surprise, as if I had said the most extraordinary thing in the world.

"To be part of the circus? To travel all the time? Not knowing whether we will have a good audience that night or not? Always tired, always working?"

Her eyes were fixed on the white wall, as if she wanted to look through it and see the inside of the house. She continued to talk, more to herself than to me.

"Every year, when we come to this town and I see this old house, with such a large, breezy porch, with a garden full of jasmine and so many other flowers that I do not know, I wonder what it would be like to live here. To go to school, to have friends that come over to visit, to sleep each night in a real bed, in the *same* real bed . . ."

Like a tennis ball in play, the surprise bounced back and forth between us. I looked at her, not understanding how she could think my life was more desirable than her own. Then she added: "That's why I come here to practice each morning. So I can pretend that I am in my own house, that I have just gotten up and eaten breakfast in the dining room, that I am outside on my own front porch. . . ."

The pail had filled as we spoke. We could hear the voice of one of the circus men calling from the other side of the street: "¡Zenaida! ¡Zenaida! ¡ZENAIDA!"

The young, agile girl raised the pail full of water as if it had no weight, and ran off with swift ballerina steps without saying good-bye. The water spilled from the pail, leaving a trail of drops on the entrance to *los framboyanes,* on the cement sidewalk, and on the road that ran between our two worlds.

Under the Royal Palms

Winner of the Pura Belpré Award

with illustrations by Edel Rodriguez

Gratefully:

To Quica,
who builds bridges out of sun beams

To Jon Lanman,
who turns dreams into books

To Rosalma,
*grateful for your unending support
and for being who you are*

Introduction

Wearing my high school uniform; each stripe represents one year

10 years old

15 years old

WHILE I WAS growing up I lived in Camagüey, the city where I was born, on the eastern part of Cuba, one of the many islands in the Caribbean Sea. The four larger islands in the Caribbean are called Greater Antilles. They include Hispaniola, the island shared by Haiti and the Dominican Republic; Puerto Rico; Jamaica; and Cuba. Of all these islands, Cuba, long and narrow, is the largest. It lies very close to the southern tip of Florida. Because Cuba is located at the entrance to the Gulf of Mexico, it is sometimes called "the Key to the Gulf." On account of its beauty, its fertile land, and its incomparable weather—never too humid nor too hot—it is also called "the Pearl of the Antilles."

When I was growing up, Camagüey was a quiet place. In Cuba we called it a city, but in a larger country it would have been called a town. Many of its streets were narrow and winding, and most were paved with stones. After a rain, the gray stones were slippery and dangerous for the horses that pulled the carts of the milkmen, the bakers, and the coal vendors. It upset me deeply whenever I saw a horse slip and fall on the wet stones.

Not many people had private cars. Most used public transportation: crowded buses, or slow and noisy streetcars called *tranvías*. We also probably walked much more than most people in the United States do today, to go to school or to work, to go shopping, or to visit relatives or friends in the afternoon, something we often did without giving them notice and a custom we all welcomed.

The majority of the houses had tile roofs, with gutters to gather the rainwater. The colonial houses in the center of town were spacious, usually built around a central courtyard, with large doors and windows that went from ceiling to floor and were protected by carved wooden railings.

It was a city of contrasts. Contrasts in the way people behaved, in their beliefs and in their practices. Although most people would have called Cuba a Catholic country, in reality there were people from many religious traditions. The African people who had been kept in slavery used many Catholic symbols and images to continue practicing their own beliefs under the cover of Catholicism. A few people had become Protestants, following the preaching of various American missionaries: Episcopalian, Baptist, Methodist, Adventist. There have always been Jewish people in Spanish-speaking countries, and many more arrived in Cuba fleeing Europe during World War II. Chinese people had been lured to Cuba with the promise of free land. After long years of indentured work on the fields, their perseverance and hard work had allowed most of them to settle in the cities where they owned stores, restaurants, laundry services, or vegetable gardens. Although some of them adopted Christian beliefs, many retained their ancestral religious practices. And then there were the freethinkers, maybe the fewest in number, who believed that spirituality need not be expressed under any specific set of rules.

There was a small, economically powerful circle of landowners, cattle ranchers, and professionals who observed European customs and considered themselves more refined. They listened to classical music, went to fine art exhibitions, and longed for theater and ballet. They spoke with controlled voices that displayed their education.

And then there was a much greater number of working people, mostly strong, loud, and boisterous, filled with energy and life, whose education was very different from that provided by the schools—theirs was the education of home traditions and long-held beliefs.

The most striking contrasts for me were not the differences in education and beliefs. The largest, most significant contrast was that some had so much—and others had very little. While for some life was easy, almost a paradise on this beautiful island, for others the struggle to stay alive was extremely demanding. Many, especially young children, did not survive.

Even as a young child, these contrasts confused and concerned me. Because Cuba was a very young republic—it had won its independence from Spain in 1889 and from the U.S.

in 1902, less than forty years before I was born—I heard many stories of the struggle for independence, of the dreams that had inspired the struggle, and of the heroes who had led the way. And I looked around me to see if those ideals were indeed alive, only to be saddened when I realized that in most ways, they were not. In the countryside, the majestic royal palms towered above the surrounding trees. But beneath those palms I saw too much poverty and too much pain, and I knew that the realization of the dreams of justice and equality were still far away.

My own family was not among the more affluent, but the hard work of many family members who shared our large house kept us from suffering the needs of those who had so little. Yet this was a constant cause of concern and struggle within me. Although very early on I began to realize that real wealth did not lie in material things, my heart was still saddened by those who suffered so much just to survive.

It moved me to know that the old Quinta Simoni, which I loved so dearly and which was a world of my own, had also been where the young patriot Ignacio Agramonte and his beloved Amalia Simoni had met, spent time together, and briefly lived after their marriage. Later, Ignacio was killed in battle, and his ashes were scattered because the Spanish government did not want his tomb to become a shrine. For me, the garden where he had strolled with Amalia, the porch where they had exchanged sweet words of love and shared their dreams for an independent Cuba, were indeed a shrine to their ideals.

My beloved *abuelita* Lola explained those ideals of freedom and equality to me every evening during the few years we shared. Later, after her death, the house became for us a shrine to her memory. I am sharing some of the feelings and memories of my childhood, as well as some of the stories that were told to me, as a way of keeping these memories alive and continuing to understand life. I have called the following collection *Under the Royal Palms* because the royal palm, standing majestic and alone, rising above the trees that surround it, is the symbol of an independent Cuba.

I hope that you will see my stories as an invitation for you to discover the many stories in your own life, and the meaning that they hold for you.

Chapter 1
The Bats

Two photos of my grandmother Lola

Abuelita Lola y abuelito Medardo

La Quinta Simoni

DAILY LIFE IN La Quinta Simoni started at a very early hour. The soothing night fragrances of jasmine and gardenia, which entered my bedroom from the garden, were quickly overtaken by the acrid but friendly smell of coffee brewing.

Very soon everyone would be bustling about, getting ready to leave—my father to teach at the high school, tío Tony to the radio station, tío Medardito to his office, tía Lolita to her classes, and abuelita Lola to the school she ran.

Before long, the big house was all my mother's and mine. While she worked on her bookkeeping ledgers, I would spend hours playing outside, under the trees, by myself.

Every afternoon, around four o'clock, I had to take a bath and get dressed "for the evening." I would set aside the boots I hated, with their hard insoles to support my flat feet, and put on my white shoes with a little strap on top and a buckle on the side. As my mother tied the bow at the back of my dress, I felt like a butterfly, forced daily to return to her chrysalis, and daily freed again.

The next thing to be done each afternoon was to gather *maravillas*. These simple wild flowers—red, orange, white, purple, or speckled—opened late in the day. It was as if, like me, they led two lives: one curled up and wrinkled during the heat of the day, another open and splendid in the late afternoon as the sun began to set. They grew plentifully on an empty lot about half a block from the old Quinta Simoni. I would walk proudly down the sidewalk, glancing at my shoes, ready to gather as many flowers as I could.

On my return, my grandmother would be waiting for me on the front porch, sitting in a rocking chair, ready to praise the beauty of my simple offering. Then we would both go on tiptoes, as if approaching an altar, to place the flowers on top of the piano, a ritual that pleased us both. We made garlands to wrap around the bust of José Martí, the beloved Cuban poet who contributed greatly to the struggle for independence. We also placed garlands at the feet of a doll wearing typical Mayan dress that someone had brought my grandmother from Guatemala. Abuelita would smile and say, "For Martí and his *niña de Guatemala*." I would smile, too, because the poem that Martí had written for a young girl in Guatemala, although very sad, was one of my favorites. And I loved that my grandmother had decided to unite, on top of her piano, the poet and the girl who had died loving him.

Once the ritual was finished, we would walk hand in hand out to the large front porch with its high masonry arches. She would sit in the rocking chair, and I would sit on the steps

a few feet away, listening to her sing verses set to music she
herself had composed:

> *Quiero a la sombra de un ala*
> *contar este cuento en flor,*
> *la niña de Guatemala*
> *la que se murió de amor.*

> Under the shadow of a wing,
> I will let this story blossom,
> of a young Guatemalan girl,
> who died of a broken heart.

The setting sun would turn the sky bright orange, and my
grandmother would begin a new song:

> *Cultivo una rosa blanca*
> *en junio como en enero,*
> *para el amigo sincero*
> *que me da su mano franca.*
> *Y para el cruel, que me arranca*
> *el corazón con que vivo,*
> *cardos ni ortigas cultivo,*
> *cultivo una rosa blanca.*

> I tend with care a white rose

both in January and in June
for the true friend
who offers a sincere hand.
And for the cruel one
who tears out my beating heart
I tend neither thistles nor thorns,
I tend with care a white rose.

The night would fall quickly around us, without giving much notice, as it does in the tropics. Then the first bats would appear. They lived above the porch, between the ceiling and the roof. We never saw or heard them during the day. But at nightfall their squeaks began, like an orchestra tuning its instruments before a concert, and it was as if the ceiling itself came alive.

Occasionally, a little one would fall to the floor through a crack in the ceiling, either pushed by a thoughtless adult or as a result of its own carelessness. Even though it was not ready to fly yet, by instinct the little bat would open its membranous wings, glide down, and land alive, although perhaps a bit stunned. Sometimes an adult bat would come immediately to the rescue. Then the little one would cling to the adult's chest and enjoy a safe return home. But on occasions when no adult came, we had to decide whether to fetch the tall ladder and try to place the baby back in the nest, or to keep it in a shoe box and feed it with my doll's bottle. Fortunately for the bats, this only happened once in a while.

Most nights, my grandmother and I would pretend to count the bats as they left their nest to feed on the fruit from our backyard: sweet mangoes, guavas, soft and delicious *nísperos*. We knew from the start that it was impossible to keep a true tally, because in a few minutes their number would increase from a handful circling over our heads to many dozens, coming and going, so that we were unable to tell which were the ones just leaving the nest. Counting them over and over again, we would finally give up and burst out laughing at the bats, at ourselves, at our game, and at the delightful warmth of the night, fragrant with the aroma of jasmine and gardenias. My aunts and my mother would smile and shake their heads: "There go those two, counting bats again. . . ."

The quiet serenity of those evenings and the tender love my grandmother and I shared has nourished me throughout my life. On the many occasions when I have been engaged in an impossible task and felt that, once again, I was trying to count bats, I have allowed myself to laugh. Some of the best things in life are like counting bats: It was never the final count that mattered, but rather the joy of seeing them fly.

Chapter 2
Clay

Playing by the árbol de carolinas

IN THE SUMMER months, rain would often pour unannounced, pounding furiously on the treetops, the roof, and the soil. These summer rains provided wonderful fun for my mother and me as we would run outside in our bathing suits to play. It was wonderful to feel the strong drops on my bare back, to shake my head and feel my long hair wet and heavy with rainwater, to take off my rubber sandals and let the soft mud ooze between my toes.

But as much as I enjoyed the mud, I much preferred the clay, thick and red, which I gathered across the river to make toy dishes and cups. I would roll the clay into a ball and then press it between the palms of my hands until it became a round dish. To make a soup bowl, I would press hard in the center of a clay ball with both thumbs. I would make a cup by pressing a ball of softened clay against the palm of one hand to flatten the base. Then, with my index finger, I would slowly form a round cavity in the center. The handle was a cylinder of clay, bent to create the right shape.

Usually I let my creations dry in the sun. But occasionally, *los alfareros,* the brick makers who worked on the other side of the river, would let me put my own board, with my carefully made dishes, inside their oven. Sometimes the dishes would crack in the oven's strong heat, but some survived as the red clay turned black, strong, and durable.

Not just a plaything for a child, that same red clay was used for many useful products. Camagüey is well known for its *tinajones,* huge round-bellied clay pots. During colonial times, when there was no town water reservoir, every courtyard had at least one *tinajón.* In the rainy season, rainwater would stream down from the high tile roofs into the gutters, to be collected in the *tinajones* and preserved for the months in which there was no rain. Nowhere else in Cuba could such superb clay be found, nor were other potters able to create pots of that size. Those potters had all but disappeared by the time of my childhood, but the clay, red and thick, was still abundant.

The few potters who still remained, turning their potter wheels with bare feet while wetting the clay that took form beneath their hands, made only little *tinajones.* These souvenirs were sold to the few tourists who visited Camagüey, and especially to nostalgic former residents who had moved to La Habana and wanted to decorate their new houses with memories of the land of their youth.

The little *tinajones,* or *tinajoncitos,* were sold in different styles and sizes. Some were simply made of fired clay, others were glazed, and still others were painted with small landscapes—perhaps a solitary palm tree standing by a *bohío,* a thatched-roof cottage.

As children, many of us carried a *porrón* to school every day. This round clay jug had a carrying handle on top; a small opening to fill it with water on one side; and on the other, a spout to drink from in the heat of the day, as the clay kept the water wonderfully cool. Time often brings changes quickly. The *porrón* was one of the things that I saw disappear during my own childhood. My sister, Flor, is only seven years younger than I, but she never carried a *porrón* to school. Instead, she drank from a water fountain.

I have forgotten much of what I learned in school as a child. But how vividly I remember the lessons I learned from clay! Softening clay was a tedious job, but I could only mold it if it was soft enough. Nothing could speed the process. Although water helped, one had to use just the right amount; too much would make the clay slippery and impossible to form. Working with clay taught me patience.

Since I could only use the brick maker's oven occasionally, most of my little pots dried in the sun, which left them fragile, but for that reason all the more precious. The things I shaped from clay taught me to treasure what I can create.

I have grown up to love pottery. Whenever I see a clay pot, I think of the women who, throughout thousands of years, have molded clay in their hands to carry water, to store food, to cook for and nourish their families. I like to wonder about the first human being to ever discover that clay could be shaped by human hands, along with the many others who, in different parts of the world, arrived at the same discovery.

To me, life is a series of miracles, and the presence of this generous and elemental material around us—ready to be used for so many purposes, ready to be made into a thing of beauty—is one of those miracles.

How fresh and cool the water from the *porrón* tasted—pure water, with a slight flavor of clay! Water that had trickled through the stone filter in our kitchen as we slept. Water that my mother had lovingly poured for me that morning. A little bit of home for the long school hours. Friendly water, always waiting for us right next to our desks during the heat of the day.

Chapter 3
Explorers

Mamá and tía Mireya as children, by the river Tínima

With tío Mario, tía Lolita, and a cousin from La Habana on the grounds of La Quinta Simoni

LIFE AT LA Quinta Simoni provided constant invitations for adventure. One morning, I met my cousins Jorge and Virginita by the fallen tree. It was a huge poplar, possibly uprooted by a hurricane. But the tree had refused to die and, although fallen, it had sprouted new branches. These new branches, covered with heart-shaped leaves, projected upward like spears pointed at the sky.

The tree was an excellent place for playing. Sometimes it became our pirate ship: On it, we crossed the Caribbean while the wind filled our green sails. At other times it was a castle, and from its turrets we defended our fortress from invading warriors. Or perhaps it was a covered wagon crossing the plains, or a sleigh racing across the Russian steppes pursued by a wolf pack. On this day, the fallen tree was our camp in the middle of the jungle, and from there we planned to go exploring.

Jorge instructed us on the importance of moving silently, crawling through the bushes to evade the ferocious predators and fierce warriors who followed us. We were not to speak or ever to look behind us. If we dawdled or turned back, we might be eaten by wild beasts or captured by headhunters.

Virginita and I listened to him, fascinated. Not only was

he two years older than his sister and four years older than I, he was the one who read the adventure stories that we all later reenacted. We trusted his words completely and followed him without hesitation.

We left behind the fallen tree and the chicken coop, where the hens were bathing themselves in the dust and eating the red berries from the *ateje* tree. We crept through the shadows of the flame trees, across the brilliant crimson carpet of their fallen petals, until we made it to the river.

We encountered no wild beasts or headhunters on our journey. On the contrary, our arrival merely prompted a few frogs and a *jicotea,* a river turtle that had been sunning itself on a rock, to jump into the water.

We crossed the river without any difficulty and sneaked around *el tejar,* the brick maker's place. The old brick maker, *el alfarero,* and his two sons, who had come from Spain after the Spanish Civil War, paid no attention to us. They were working barefooted. Their white trousers, which were made from flour sacks, were covered with red clay. Their suntanned backs glistened with sweat. They were trying to loosen the iron wheel of *la pisa,* the round pit where the clay was broken and softened. The old skinny horse who made the wheel go around and around was waiting patiently, possibly thankful for having this brief rest under the sun.

Beyond *el tejar,* the thorn bushes began. People said that the *marabú* plant was brought to Cuba by a countess who loved its flowers, which resemble pink powder puffs. But the bush did not want to remain locked up in a garden, so it slowly spread out across the fields.

Once *marabú* takes hold of a field, it is difficult to clear it. Its roots intertwine under the soil, forming a net that is almost impossible to pull out. One must plow the field to turn over the earth and then rake it, making sure that every last piece of root is removed. Otherwise, it will sprout again.

A *marabú* field is impenetrable unless a path is opened with a machete. The thorny branches form a barrier open only at ground level.

And it was at that level that we began to cross the *marabú* field. Jorge showed us how easy it could be if we simply crawled between and around the thin trunks. It was easy enough, indeed. But soon we had lost him. Because it was impossible to stand up or even to turn, we did not stop. Virginita and I continued, trying to follow the route plotted by our chief explorer, who was by now far ahead and out of sight.

Out in the countryside, people used the *marabú* to make charcoal. At that time in Cuba, very few people had electric or gas stoves. Poor people cooked with wood. Those who could afford it used charcoal. And the *marabú* charcoal was the best. *Marabú* is a very hard wood, so its coals last a long time before they are totally consumed.

As we moved farther into the *marabú* field, the trees seemed to grow closer and closer together, the branches more intertwined. The thorns caught on our dresses, tore at our hair. But there was nothing we could do. With Jorge's order never to turn back still fresh in our minds, and with a desperate desire to escape the *marabú* jungle, we struggled on, hoping to find our leader at some turn of the maze.

The coal makers sold their charcoal on the streets. Those who were more fortunate had a *plancha,* a primitive open wagon with four big wheels and no sides, on which they would place their charcoal sacks. The poorer ones would walk through the street with a half-full sack of charcoal slung over their shoulders, selling a handful of coal for the day's cooking to those who could not afford to buy a whole sack. They wore one of the coarse burlap sacks over their heads to protect their backs from the heavy burden.

For hours, Virginita and I crawled through the *marabú,* avoiding when we could the dead thorny branches that had fallen on the ground, leaving behind pieces of our dresses and strands of our hair.

Meanwhile, at home, everyone was alarmed. The girls were lost! Jorge, who had returned a long time ago, had moved on to other pastimes. Nobody knew where to find us.

My parents went to the river. They talked to the brick makers. But not for a minute did they imagine we would have entered the *marabú* field. Jorge, to avoid a scolding, said only that he had left us playing at the other side of the river.

Late in the afternoon, with our clothes in tatters and our

faces covered with muddy tears, we finally emerged at the other end of the *marabú* field. We were immediately surrounded by a group of children, half naked and as covered with dirt as we were by then. They invited us to play hide-and-seek, but we were much too exhausted to accept.

Hearing us crying, the parents of the children appeared at the doors of their huts.

"*¡Pobrecitas!* Poor little ones," one of the women said kindly. "They are lost." She took me in her arms and asked Virginita to follow her.

With water from an old tin basin, she washed our faces and arms, all covered with scratches. Then she opened an old lard can, which she used as her cupboard, and took out two crackers—thick, large sailors' crackers. She sprinkled them with coarse brown sugar—poor people's way of fooling their bodies into believing they had eaten when there was no more substantial food to be had. Then she gave one to each of us.

"Eat, little ones, eat," she said, coaxing us. "Don't worry. We'll take you home."

From the doorway, the children looked at us with big, open eyes, trying to imagine what we possibly could have done to merit such a generous and unexpected treat.

Chapter 4
Broken Wings

Above: two photos of tío Medardito

Tía Mireya, Mamá, abuelita Lola, tío Medardito, tía Lolita, and tía Virginia

Tío Medardito and his wife, Geraldina

The hearse ready to take Medardito to the cemetery

My MOTHER HAD three sisters but only one brother, Medardo. To distinguish him from his father, abuelito Medardo, he was called Medardito by the family. All four sisters were so outgoing, athletic, and daring, at a time when most women were not expected to be, that perhaps Medardito felt the need to live up to their example. Or maybe it was simply because he had been born with a surprisingly tall and strong body that Medardito grew up to excel in sports and succeed in all physical challenges. At a time when movies and comic books extolled such heroes, tío Medardito seemed to all of us to be a mixture of Tarzan and Superman.

Several times, he had braved the currents of the flooded Río Tínima to save someone from its muddy waters. He was the delight of the neighborhood boys because he would give them rides on his large, nickel-chromed bicycle, six or seven at a time: one on the handlebars, one or two on the bar in front of him, two or three on the grill behind his seat, and, most daring of all, one perched on his shoulders. He would ride at full speed, as if he did not have to balance this human tower, and the boys would scream with delight and beg for yet another ride.

At other times, people riding the bus as it crossed the bridge over the Tínima would gasp with surprise and fear when they saw him on the high bridge, walking precariously on the railing like a circus acrobat.

Medardito loved adventures and wanted to explore any new frontier. Yet there was so little excitement in Camagüey! When he was twenty-four years old, he decided to learn to fly an airplane. He convinced a friend to join him, and each of them bought his own "flying machine," a primitive two-person plane, with a single motor and a precarious frame of light wood and canvas.

Medardo was by then married to his young bride, Geraldina, a beautiful brunette whom everyone said resembled Deanna Durbin, a Hollywood star at that time. They lived, as we did, in the big old Quinta Simoni. Their only child, my cousin Nancy, had just recently been born.

Neither his wife, nor my mother, nor my younger *tía* Lolita wanted Medardito to fly. My father tried to point out to him the risks involved. Manolo Díaz, tía Lolita's husband, who I called tío Tony, made every effort to divert him whenever Medardo came home from his work at a downtown office. But nothing could deter my uncle from the excitement that he felt while soaring, first behind the instructor, and then very soon afterward all by himself—rising above the red tile roofs and the winding streets that had so restricted his world, gliding like the mighty *auras,* the Cuban buzzards, over the plains where the royal palms stood majestically.

By the time Medardito got off from work on weekdays, it was usually too late to go flying. But on weekends, he never missed a single opportunity.

So, while he lived for the weekends, the rest of the family dreaded those Saturdays and Sundays. Secretly, without wanting to admit it, I longed for the weekends, too. To me, what my uncle was doing was exciting. I felt both pride and joy that he would dare to defy everyone and everything, including the force of gravity that keeps us all tied to the earth.

I had never been on an airplane, and it would be many years before I would fly. The closest I had come to flying was when my father pushed me hard on a swing he had tied to the high branch of a tree in the backyard. Or when, on clear nights, my father would place a blanket on *la azotea,* the flat rooftop, and we would quietly gaze at the stars until it seemed that we too were floating in the galaxy. Oh, but to *really* fly! I could easily understand why tío Medardito would not give it up.

Torn between her fear and her own pride, my mother had agreed to embroider his jumpsuit with a pair of wings and his monograph, MLS, for Medardo Lafuente Salvador. The day had been dark and cloudy, as if a storm were approaching, and my mother and aunts had sighed with relief, thinking that at least that day he would not go flying.

But in the afternoon the sky cleared, and tío Medardito was determined to take wing.

My mother, busy at the sewing machine, kept arguing with

him. He must wait patiently, she said, for her to finish the complicated embroidery on the back of the jumpsuit. But even I could see through her subtle ploy to keep him home. Medardito finally prevailed and forced her to give him the jumpsuit with only half of the embroidery done. "What I want is to fly." He tried to reassure her with a kiss. "You can finish the embroidery during the week."

A moment later, he jumped on a bus for the long trip to the airport at the other end of town. I played for a while, until my mother reminded me to take the shower that was part of my afternoon ritual. Then I could go out and sit on the porch, or collect flowers to make garlands, or wait for the neighborhood children who came to our porch to play.

But this afternoon there would be no games. I had only been in the bath for a few minutes, my body all covered with soap, my hair held high atop my head in a white cloud of shampoo, when I heard a noise like nothing I had ever heard. It was a thunder of human voices and running feet.

I climbed on the toilet seat to look out the bathroom window. There were hundreds of people running along the road in front of our house, heading toward the river. Everyone was shouting at once, so I could not understand what they were saying. But I did not wait. Without rinsing or drying myself, I put on the same dress I had just taken off and ran out barefoot.

Instead of going out into the street—the number of people there was frightening—I ran in the same direction, but behind the house, through the courtyard, down the lane lined with flame trees, and through the garden my great-grandmother loved so much.

By then I had figured out where everyone was heading and why. We were running in the same direction as an approaching plane, a plane that each moment grew larger as it loomed closer and closer to the ground, with a loud noise that was not the usual steady purr of a functioning motor, but the coughing and spitting of a motor incapable of holding the plane in the air.

As the plane passed above my head, I could see the big numbers and letters painted on the wings. It was NOT my uncle's plane! And yet, I kept running with the same energy, trampling the rosebushes that my great-uncle Manuel had cultivated to sell on the city streets, tearing my dress on the thorns.

And I was the first to reach the plane after the deafening impact. I was followed closely by my father, who quickly took me in his arms and pulled me away, but not before my eyes had filled with the terrible image I still remember today.

Papá knew immediately there was nothing that could be done for my uncle, whose face had crashed forward against the control panel. His instinct was to protect me, to protect my mother, who was there now, wailing—how can someone cry with so much pain and anguish and horror!—and my younger aunt, Lolita, who was holding her pregnant belly as if about to faint.

There were many hands to help lift the lifeless body from

the plane. My *tía* Geraldine, until that afternoon my uncle's wife and now his widow, was ushered into a car to hold on her lap the beloved head now unrecognizable.

How long and dark was that unbearable afternoon! The house was swarming with people. Some we knew, many were well-wishers wanting to bring some comfort, but most were just curious onlookers.

To many in town, we had always been an odd family. Living in a house reputedly haunted, all of us were looked upon as eccentric. Abuelito Medardo was loved by his students and well-respected in intellectual circles. But to the ordinary people, he was an odd gentleman who spoke as if reciting poetry and always walked with a book in his hand. They told funny anecdotes of having seen him so engrossed in his book as he walked that, upon bumping into a lamppost, he raised his hat, said "Excuse me," and continued walking.

An odd family, indeed. My grandmother Lola had been the first woman in town to cut her hair in a short page-boy fashion. That was unheard of in a grown woman with children, and a school principal at that. And my mother and my aunts had not only cut their hair too, they had also shortened their skirts and exposed their bare legs without stockings. They rode horses bareback, and drove motorcycles, cars, and trucks.

Yes, indeed, we were odd. We were not even Catholic, in a town that was almost exclusively so. And it was not because we were Jewish or Protestant, either. My grandparents had simply chosen to believe in freedom of thought and spirit.

Now, to top it all off, my uncle had dared to fly one of those flying machines and . . . he had crashed!

No one held any grudges against us. We were known to be kind and generous. Even though any kindness was always shown quietly, people knew they could count on us.

But now, their curiosity had been stirred up. And there they were, the whole town, to see, to examine, to explore, to probe, to judge. . . . People whom we did not know felt they could enter the house. No space was sacred to them, no privacy was respected. This accident, and the grief that had torn the fabric of our own lives, became a spectacle like a circus.

My mother and my aunts cried loudly, wailing, letting their pain fill the house from which all joy had disappeared in an instant.

Five years earlier, abuelito Medardo had died a painful but serenely accepted death, with his wife and children gathered around his bed. In his own room, he said good-bye as gently as he had always lived. He had simply asked for three teaspoons of water, saying, "For me, the time is here."

Two years later, my dear *abuelita* Lola had followed him, going peacefully in her sleep. In both instances, large crowds had come to the wake, waiting outside the house behind the black hearse pulled by black horses with tall black feather tufts, following it on foot all the way to the distant *camposanto*, the "holy field," or cemetery.

On both previous occasions, the crowds had been like the full and gentle swelling of the river after the summer rains. Now the mob was like the flood after a hurricane: uncontrollable, turbulent, sweeping away everything in its path.

Papá and tío Tony were both stunned, having just lost their best friend. They were beset by the guilt of not having known how to prevent this disaster that all had feared. All their attention was now on their wives. Papá, looking after my baby sister, Flor, who was still nursing, worried that my mother's milk would dry up. At a time when baby formula was not common, this was considered disastrous. Tío Tony worried about his pregnant wife, tía Lolita. And both were bewildered about what to do with Geraldina, the young widow, who alternated between expressions of utmost grief and a pale and stiff rigidity in which she herself looked like death.

All over the house, people were trying to explain the accident in the most bizarre ways. The truth, which I learned later, was that because tío Medardito was delayed so long on the bus, his friend had decided to go ahead and fly by himself. But once aboard his own plane, he had trouble starting it. Thinking that Medardito was not going to show up at all, he went ahead and borrowed my uncle's plane. When Medardito got to the airfield, he found his plane gone. Believing it to be a prank, he took his friend's plane instead. This time the plane started fine, only to malfunction in midair.

Why did he choose the rose field next to our house for his

crash landing? Some people believed that he was showing off, that he had wanted to impress his wife. Most likely, he wanted to spare the town. He knew this field well. And yes, in moments of great despair, maybe one does try to get close to home.

For me, the speculation was useless and hurtful. What did it really matter? The unthinkable had happened. And my grief was heightened by my own unbearable secret. I could still hear my mother and my aunts repeating, over and over, between their bursts of sobbing and wailing, "We never wanted him to go," "We did all we could to dissuade him," "We tried to make him stop flying."

But only I knew that *I* had not wanted him to stop. Just that afternoon I had secretly rejoiced in seeing him so determined, overruling everyone in order to go out to his plane.

There was no possible consolation. I felt guilty, as if I had been the one to send him to his death. Of course, I had never believed that flying was as dangerous as everyone else seemed to think. But why had I not seen it? How could I have wanted him to fly when it was going to cause such pain?

What I did then is something I have kept secret for many years. I am telling it now because sharing one's hidden sorrows, those thoughts that we sometimes believe to be shameful, is a way to begin to heal our wounds. I am sharing this because as we hear each other's stories, we often begin to understand ourselves better and to feel less alone.

Riddled by my feelings of guilt, I rushed into my room, a

room now invaded by strangers, and grabbed Heidi, my precious doll, named after the protagonist of my favorite book.

This doll was my truest friend. Heidi slept with me, kept me company, listened to all my thoughts and dreams. I carried her with me always, sharing every moment with her as two best friends would.

Now I ran with her in my arms to the back of the house. I knew my father's carpenter's bench well, and finding a hammer was not difficult. In the large courtyard, squatting behind the large masonry turret which led to the *aljibe,* the water cellar where rainwater was collected in colonial times, I placed Heidi on the tiled floor and smashed her head with the hammer, breaking that sweet little round forehead I had kissed so many times before, just as the plane's control panel had shattered my uncle's skull.

I hid the broken doll among the bushes, covering her small body with my tears and flower petals. Then I sat down next to one of the columns in the courtyard and silently cried myself to sleep.

I don't know who found me that night, or when or how I was taken to town. But the next day, I found myself at my *abuelito* Modesto's house, walking aimlessly in the backyard.

I had forgotten all that had happened the day before, yet I felt the most powerful urge to go back to my own home. Tío Mario, who had been left in charge of me, was not hard to persuade.

But getting back was a nightmare. All of the buses were packed with people heading in only one direction. Our sleepy town, where nothing ever happened, had been shaken by what was probably the most unexpected event since the War of Independence. When we finally arrived, the house was so full of people that only by crawling between their legs could I enter. Every horror of the previous day was now magnified in front of me.

I stopped at the door of the room where my uncle's body lay. There were my two older cousins, Jorge and Virginita. They had just arrived from La Habana with their mother, Virginia, my oldest aunt. Tía Virginia had joined her sisters at their brother's side, while my two cousins, like me, had not been able to enter the room where our mothers cried incessantly.

I held fast to each of them with both hands. I was shaking from fear and pain, and sweating from the efforts of pushing past so many people to get into my own house. I led in silence, and they followed me outside with the solidarity of our love and our mutual pain. Once outdoors, I pulled out my beloved doll from beneath the few leaves and petals I had used to cover her the night before. As I sat on the grass, rocking the broken doll one last time, my cousin Virginita put her arm around my shoulder while Jorge, having taken a shovel from the garden toolshed, dug the small grave. They wordlessly accepted the broken doll, just as they had accepted my uncle's death with a stunned silence.

We shrouded the little body in a pillowcase. Virginita covered the bottom of the grave with flowers and Jorge placed the doll inside. Virginita and I brought some jasmine, carnations, and a few roses from the courtyard flower beds. Jorge continued to fill the grave with dirt until there was no more sign of Heidi, now forever lost to me in body, reduced to memory, just like our uncle.

Her softness and his strength, her smallness and his height, her silent acceptance of my kisses and his boisterous laughter while he lifted me up in the air, her quiet company and his exhilarating playfulness, all were now gone. Never again would I hold Heidi on my lap as I read a book beneath the flame trees, nor would I ride on my uncle's shoulders so high that I could pick the blossoms from those tall branches. And yet today, how alive in my memory are both my sweet gentle doll, sacrificed by a hurting child, and my brave uncle, inviting me, every morning, to the untold adventure of a brand-new day.

Chapter 5

Christmas for All

With my violin at Joyería El Sol, my parents' jewelry store

My sister, Flor, and me wearing our school uniforms

My sister, Flor

UNTIL I WAS eight years old, my mother worked as an accountant for several small businesses. She would visit each store, collect the large ledgers and the voluminous envelopes filled with receipts, and bring them home. There she would spend many hours a day copying figures into the ledgers with her meticulous handwriting and adding the long columns of numbers. Then she would return the thick ledgers and envelopes and collect new ones from her next client.

My mother was very proud of her profession. She had completed her education going to school at night after I was born, and was very proud of being one of the first women to be certified as a public accountant in Cuba.

After my sister, Flor, was born, my mother decided that she was ready to have her own business. She rented a garage from a typewriter repair shop in Calle Avellaneda and opened a small store where she sold buttons and lace, scissors and thread, needles and yarn as well as paper, pencils, pens, and erasers. Customers tended to come to the store at certain hours. Women came in the morning, on their way home from the market. Students came in the afternoon, right after being let out from school. Young women came later, on their way to night classes. No matter who they were, my mother always had a word of wisdom or encouragement for them, or a joke to make them laugh. Sometimes I suspect the customers came into the little store more for my mother's words than for the little trinkets they bought—especially the young women who came for a pad of paper or a pencil, but also asked my mother to go over their homework or explain a difficult math problem.

In the quiet hours of midday, my mother kept doing her accounting work, leaning on the counter while she waited for a customer to come in—a lady to browse among the lace, a harried maid to select a zipper, or a young boy to buy a jar of glue to make a kite.

My baby sister, Florecita, was kept in a large cardboard box which served as a makeshift playpen, and I did my homework sitting on the tile floor, grateful for its coolness in the hot afternoon.

One evening at dinner, back home at La Quinta Simoni, my mother surprised everyone. My parents had been speaking for some time now with tía Lolita and tío Tony about how difficult it was for them, as two young couples, to keep up the big house. Within the span of only seven years, both my grandparents and tío Medardito had died. My other two aunts, tía Virginia and tía Mireya, had gone to live and work in La Habana. And the big old house was expensive to maintain.

But now my mother had a novel idea. She suggested that they could all pool their savings to purchase an old jewelry store that was for sale in the center of town. The portion of the rent they would get from La Quinta Simoni would help pay for the rent of the jewelry store building, and we could all live in back of the store.

It did not take long to convince the others. Here was an opportunity to have a business and to live on the premises. That would ease the economic situation. Also, I suspect that the large, rambling Quinta Simoni reminded them of how much they missed those who were no longer living with us.

So, shortly afterward, we moved to Calle República—to the house behind the *Joyería El Sol*, a few blocks away from the little store that had been my mother's first business venture.

For me, it was a most difficult time. I loved the old Quinta Simoni, where I had been born. I loved its large rooms with high ceilings, and the flat roof, where my father and I would lie gazing at the night sky while he told me stories about the constellations. I loved the pigeons and guinea pigs my aunt Lolita raised, and above all, I loved my friends the flame trees, with their gnarled roots where I sat as if in the lap of my grandfather.

I realized that perhaps the house made the adults sad, after the deaths of abuelito Medardo, abuelita Lola, and my young *tío* Medardito. But for me, they were still alive. I felt their presence in the hallways, on the porch, and in the courtyard. All during the four years in which we lived in the city, I longed to return to live among the trees.

The only good times in the city, for me at least, were the

Fiesta de San Juan in June, which was celebrated almost like a Mardi Gras, and of course *Las Navidades,* or Christmastime.

As soon as they bought the *Joyería El Sol,* my family began to make improvements to the old jewelry store. My father, always ready to learn new things, learned how to fix watches. My mother, lover of innovations, had the storefront redone with large display cases. She also began to display a wider variety of merchandise.

The old jewelry and stopwatches were relegated to a few special counters. The other displays were filled with porcelain and crystal. During the first Christmas season, my mother brought in toys and the traditional figurines used to create Nativity scenes.

It was a Cuban tradition, also widespread in Spain and other Latin-American countries, to set up a Nativity scene in the house during the month of December. It was a tradition shared by rich and poor alike, although the elaborateness of the scene varied greatly from home to home. More than a family's economic status, it was their willingness to make an effort, to set aside space, and to be creative that determined the size and originality of the scene.

A mountainous backdrop could be constructed with cardboard boxes covered with paper grocery sacks. The sand for the desert was brought in from a trip to the beach. The fields could be created by sprouting wheat in small cans or jars; a piece of broken mirror provided the surface for a lake. The figurines, though—the shepherds and their lambs, the three Wise Men, Mary, Joseph, and Jesus, the donkey and the cow—were usually store-bought.

My mother imported some figurines from Spain. They were made of clay and set in elaborately detailed and realistic settings carved out of cork. We cherished unpacking them, carefully lifting them from layers and layers of straw to discover the minute details of a kitchen with an old woman by the fire, a mother breast-feeding her baby, a young girl spinning wool. Each one was a unique, handmade piece. But these figurines were very expensive, and very few people could afford them.

My mother then set out to find another source. In La Habana she discovered an Italian artist who produced beautiful ceramic figurines. I still remember his name, Quirico Benigni, because he was the first Italian I had ever met. His figurines were carefully crafted, but they were made in series, not individually, so they were somewhat less expensive.

Even so, many people came into the store and handled the figurines, observed their beauty with a smile, but returned them to the shelves after seeing the price. And there were those who would not even enter the store, but simply looked longingly through the windows.

Then my father sprang into action. Though we were not Catholic, he understood the joy people found in re-creating the Nativity scenes. He saw this as a creative project in which every member of a family, young or old, could participate. And he decided we, too, would have our own family project, one that would help make Nativity figurines accessible to all.

First he enlisted tía Lolita's artistic talent and had her model in clay each of the major figures of the Nativity scene: Mary, Joseph, the Baby, the three Wise Men, the donkey, and the cow. Then he constructed a series of hinged wooden boxes, each a little bigger than the figurines. He filled one side of each box with plaster of Paris. Before the plaster hardened, he took one of the clay figurines, covered it with grease, and submerged one whole side of it into the plaster.

Once the plaster hardened, he removed the clay model, which had left an imprint in the plaster. He then repeated the same procedure with the other side of the box, and the other side of the model.

Through this simple process, he created a series of molds. Now we could grease the inside of each mold, close and lock the hinges, and pour in soft plaster of paris through a hole in the bottom of each box.

My father made several attempts until he determined how much time the plaster needed to harden in the molds. Then he was ready to operate. Several times a day, he would open his molds and take out the white figurines, which he set out to finish drying on the patio wall.

Every evening, after the little ones—my sister, Flor, and cousin Mireyita—had gone to sleep, the whole family would gather together to work on the figurines.

It was my duty to clean with a knife the excess plaster that collected along the figurines' sides, where the two halves of the mold had met. My mother then gave them a first coat of paint that colored Mary's mantle blue, the robes of the Wise Men red or green, the shepherd's cassocks brown.

Lastly, tía Lolita carefully painted their features with small brushes until the white plaster was all covered and the figurines became recognizable characters.

Tío Tony would prepare the plaster, clean the molds, and more than anything else, entertain us all with his unending stories.

The next day, some humble hands would happily exchange a few pennies for one of the figurines, which we had placed on a table by the door of the store, and take it home to add to their Nativity scene.

The pennies barely covered the cost of the materials, let alone the time spent by my parents or my aunt. In fact, the figurines were not very artistic, nor terribly graceful, I must confess. But we saw them go with the hope that they would bring others the same joy we had shared as we labored into the night together, believing that this was the essence of Christmas: a celebration in which all can take part, and find a way to express their love for one another.

Chapter 6
Gilda

Posing for the camera on my fifth birthday

Gilda

The Teatro Principal in Camagüey,
where Gilda danced

SCHOOL BECAME ENJOYABLE for me for the first time at
the beginning of fourth grade, thanks to my teacher, Gladys
Carnero. Gentle, loving, and interesting, her enthusiasm for
teaching made us all want to learn.

When midway through the school year she moved to La
Habana, I felt lost. Then I became sick. First I caught one cold
after another, then the measles, and finally the mumps. My
wonderful parents realized that something lay beneath this. The
Colegio Episcopal which I had been attending was unbearable
to me if Gladys Carnero was no longer there. So my parents
transferred me to a new school.

Although it might have been a relief had it happened at the
beginning of the school year, this transfer became another kind
of nightmare. I arrived as the new student in the middle of the
year—to a class where all of the other children had known one
another since first grade. To make it worse, at the new school,
Colegio El Porvenir, the students were seated according to their
academic performance. Those with the best grades sat in the
front; those with bad grades sat in back. Since I had no grades
yet, they sat me at the very back.

In the last row, I was surrounded mostly by boys who were

the tallest in the class. I, a year younger than my classmates, was the shortest. Furthermore, no one had discovered yet that I needed glasses. I could not see anything on the board.

And the final blow was that the two previous schools I had attended were American schools, where they taught mathematics, especially division, very differently than the Cuban schools did. So although I knew how to find the right answer, I couldn't explain how I did it. Was I ever lost!

Those first few months at the *Colegio El Porvenir* were not easy. I couldn't find any reason to be there. The teacher would write a sentence on the board, and we were supposed to analyze it, identifying the subject and the predicate, the direct object and the indirect object. We had to identify the verb tense: present perfect, past perfect, pluperfect. I would say to myself, "What is this for? How is it possible that everyone else understands it and I don't?"

I tried to hide behind one of the students who sat in front of me, but it seemed that my strategy only brought me harder questions from the teacher. "Indicative," "subjunctive," and "imperative" sounded equally horrible to me. I loved words like "zephyr" and "zenith," *"néctar"* and *"ambrosía,"* "friendship" and "loyalty." But the words "preposition," "conjunction," and "subordinate" sounded almost as ugly as "sulfur" and "hate" to me.

Because my parents had been so understanding, I felt I could not tell them how unhappy I was. There was only one thing that allowed me to survive that horrible school with its treeless cement yard—a school without songs, without drawing, without stories, without friends.

On my way to school one day, a couple of blocks down a side street that I had followed just to delay my arrival, an unexpected wisp of music greeted me, merrily escaping from a tall window behind a carved wooden railing.

On tiptoes, grasping the wooden railing, I peered inside the old colonial house from which the waltz spilled onto the street.

Inside, an enormous mirror reflected a dozen young girls in pink leotards and black slippers, practicing at the barre. At the piano an older woman played the unending waltz. In front of the class, holding a tall staff, stood a young blond woman, so pale she was almost translucent. She had incredible eyes—eyes that took in everything: the girls, the piano player, and indeed the whole room, including the far corner where a group of elegant ladies sat in mahogany rocking chairs, sleepily cooling themselves with silk fans.

As the days went by, school became bearable only because as soon as the long-awaited bell rang, I would run and cling to the window of the ballet school, imagining myself in soft slippers, changing positions, second, third, fourth, performing a *jeté* or a *plié*.

Then one afternoon the pale teacher disappeared from view, and before I realized what was happening, she was standing on the sidewalk by my side. "Do you want to study ballet? What is your name?"

Her voice was as soft as her gaze. "Come in," she said. "Come in."

Once she knew who I was, she called my mother and offered to accept me into her class. My life was changed, not only after school, but in school, too!

I was never again bothered by prepositions and conjunctions, nor by my inability to remember how much is seven times eight. Nor did I mind anymore sitting in the back of the class, although slowly, without really noticing how, I managed to move to the middle rows and even to the front.

I lived only for the moment when the bell rang and I could run to the ballet school. And it wasn't that I did very well there. I did not. I was placed at the end of the line, and there I stayed for as long as my classes continued. In spite of my love for music and for the beauty of the movements, it was as if I had three feet, or as though my left and right sides had traded places. But in spite of my clumsy attempts, so devoid of grace, how wonderful it was to be there!

No matter what mistake I made, I was never criticized nor ridiculed by Gilda, the teacher. Although I saw her become impatient once in a while, it was only when someone who could naturally do better was not paying attention. To me she offered the same gentleness she showed the youngest of the girls, looking at me with a sweet look of complicity, as if to say, "You know that I know you cannot dance, but that you long to be here, and I welcome you."

I was very surprised when one day Gilda invited me to stay after class. That was the beginning of a beautiful friendship that was cherished equally by both of us.

From that day on, at the end of class, we would go to the *saleta*, the informal sitting room and the coolest room in the house. The *saleta* opened to the courtyard, where the *tinajones*, huge clay jars, overflowed with fresh water, and jasmine filled the air with its delicate fragrance. Gilda would show me her scrapbooks filled with photos, newspaper articles, and programs, in Russian, French, and Italian. She had studied in Berlin and in Oslo with a Russian teacher, and had danced in Vienna, Munich, Amsterdam, Paris, and Rome.

Those names evoked worlds that I could barely imagine, far from the insignificant city of Camagüey. But more than the stories of ballets and parties, of triumphs and travels, I was fascinated by Gilda, by the life energy concentrated in that body, so fragile and delicate. She was to me a goddess I had the privilege to know.

At the end of the school year we had a recital at the *Teatro Principal,* and Gilda invited me to go see the theater with her before the recital. She showed me backstage, all the while telling me stories of the many theaters she had known. What an intriguing world it was backstage!

To see her dancing on the stage was a revelation. After my

ballet classmates and I concluded our simple presentation, the master of ceremonies announced a number that was not on the printed program. Gilda would interpret Stravinsky's *Firebird*. For as long as I had known her, she had always been sweet and melancholic, filled with dreams, a romantic person. Now, as she became the music on the stage, the Gilda I knew disappeared, reincarnated as passionate strength, as vibrant determination. But the beautiful dance was not to be, as she fainted on the stage, unable to finish the piece.

Someone called an ambulance, and I saw her for the last time—a wounded bird, the bright yellow lamé dress like a dying flame draped over the white gurney.

Then came the rumors. She had cancer, the horrible sickness no one wanted to mention. By now it was summer, and I did not have to go to school, but I walked the well-known route many times, stopping in front of the old colonial house whose windows now were always closed.

When I was not out walking, I lingered around the jewelry store my parents had bought when we moved to town. There, I heard Gilda had gotten married. Yet every comment related to the wedding was filled with sarcasm. "To marry Mr. Charles, who is at least forty years her senior!" "What a shame!" "How absurd!" "How obscene!" And these verbal attacks were accompanied by looks and gestures of disgust.

In our town there was never much to talk about, so any news was discussed over and over again. Whenever anyone made a comment about Gilda's wedding, I would leave and go to our house behind the store. I felt unable to reconcile her marriage to an old French professor, who had visited her occasionally and whom she treated like a father, with the romantic nostalgia she exuded as she told me of the ballets she had danced. But I was also unable to accept that anyone else had the right to criticize what they did not understand. And at a deeper level, I felt abandoned.

I longed to see Gilda, and yet I did not know how.

Soon, it became public knowledge that she was again very sick, that she was dying, that it would only take a few days. One morning I overheard my mother saying to a friend that she did not know how to tell me the bad news. That whole day I hid in the backyard, under the *guanábana* tree, so that no one would try to tell me what I already knew.

That afternoon, my parents went out. I threw myself on my bed, pretending to read a book, unable to cry for something that seemed remote and unreal, but also unable to feel, to think.

Coralia, the old woman who had been my mother's nanny, came to tell me that there was a gentleman looking for me. At ten years old, I was not used to having gentlemen callers. But on that strange day, anything was possible. Shy, uncertain of how to talk to me, Mr. Charles held his hat in his hands, his white head tipped down onto his chest.

"Are you Almita Flor? Do you know me? We have seen each other at her house, haven't we?"

Those words, "her house," so filled with love in his voice, so filled with tenderness in my memory, prevented me from uttering anything in return. Instead, I nodded.

"She asked me to bring you this," he said, as unable to use the beloved name Gilda as I was of speaking. And he took from behind his hat a photograph of Gilda, dressed as the Firebird.

"She did not want you to see her when she was so ill," he explained patiently. "She wanted you to remember her as you knew her. . . ."

And then he bent over and, hugging, we cried, the old man and the child, for the broken flight of that gentle bird we had both loved, each of us so differently and yet so truly.

Chapter 7

Madame Marie

On the streets of Camagüey, present day

IT WILL HELP bring in customers," I heard my mother telling my father. "She won't take up too much space, but above all I would like to help her, after all she has been through!"

"By all means," my father answered, "invite her to exhibit whatever she has to sell. Poor woman!"

The following day, upon returning from school to the old jewelry store, I saw the French lady. It was difficult for me to imagine that the person my parents had been talking about with such pity could be this tall woman with such a beautiful face and flaming red hair. She moved with grace and elegance behind a counter filled with embroidered tablecloths.

Little by little, I heard her story at home, piecing it together like a puzzle from a phrase heard here and a comment there.

Madame Marie, as everyone called her, was a French woman. Just before the beginning of World War II she had met a young man from Camagüey who had gone to study engineering in Paris. They had married soon afterward. Two boys were born to the couple, and they had decided to stay in France. They moved to the town where Marie's relatives lived. There they rented a large farmhouse from one of Marie's uncles. The house was surrounded by orchards, and Marie planted a vegetable garden and colorful flowers.

Being in the countryside, they were not overly concerned when the war began; but once France was occupied
by the Nazis, they became terrified. Beautiful Marie, with her
green eyes and flaming hair, was Jewish. Her father had been
Catholic, but her mother, Judith, was born Jewish, and therefore Marie was considered Jewish also. Meanwhile, the Nazis
were hunting down all Jewish people and sending them to
concentration camps.

Her husband conceived a plan. He told all of his neighbors
and relatives that he was sending his wife and children to Cuba
until the war ended. They loaded the car with suitcases and,
after saying good-bye to everyone, left in broad daylight for the
next city. But in truth, Marie and the children spent the day
hiding in the woods. That night, under the cover of darkness,
they returned home through the fields.

Her husband hid them in a closet and covered the door
with a heavy armoire. They would hide there all day long, in
case the Nazis came to search the farm. In the evening, her
husband would move the armoire so they could walk through
the dark house.

But after some time, Marie's uncle, the owner of the farm,
decided to put up another family in the house. Although he
was the brother of Marie's father, he had never accepted that his
brother had married a Jewish woman.

Now, the uncle was convinced that the French people should
collaborate with the Nazis, in order to prevent retaliation against

France. Marie's husband knew he could not trust her uncle, nor the people her uncle had brought to the farm, with his secret.

Then the situation grew worse. Once the new family had moved into the house, Felipe could no longer open the closet at all. Fortunately, he had managed to keep the room with the closet as his bedroom, but he could not move the heavy armoire without making noise. So he only dared to move it when everyone was out, and even then not for very long.

Often Marie and the two boys were locked in for days or even for weeks on end. Her husband dared only to open the little window he had cut at the back of the armoire to pass them food and to take out the waste.

During all that time, Marie taught her children their lessons. She told them all she knew about the countryside, everything about planting and gathering that she had learned as a child. She told them about the history of France, and the history of the Jewish people. Very softly she would sing lullabies to them, nursery rhymes, the love songs she had heard on the radio, the music she had danced to with her husband. And when she had sung those songs over and over, she created her own songs, about a world at peace, a land with no violence, where children were free and happy, where people united in solidarity and love for one another.

At the end of the war, once the Nazis were defeated, their horrible ordeal finally came to an end, and she was able to move to Cuba with her family.

Whenever I came back from school, Madame Marie would rub little drops of perfume behind my ears and gently squeeze my shoulder, encouraging me to go practice on the violin. "*Mon petite, mon petite,* music is a great friend," she would say to me in her caressing voice. I do not know if she ever noticed my adoring gaze as, with a soft smile curving her closed lips, she organized over and over her small display of embroidered tablecloths, napkins, and handkerchiefs in a corner of my mother's store.

Chapter 8

Uncle Manolo's Mystery

My aunt Isabel and uncle Manolo

My FATHER'S OLDER brother, my uncle Manolo Ada Rey, was a shadowy figure during the early years of my childhood. He lived in La Habana, where he had gone to study medicine. There he had married and begun his practice. Although we went to Havana twice a year, we always stayed with my mother's sister, tía Lolita, and only saw my uncle Manolo for what always felt like a very formal visit. Often, when people spoke about my uncle, the conversation seemed to be filled with long, strained silences.

In contrast to the homes of everyone else in the family, my uncle's house seemed gloomy to me. It was in the old part of town, commonly known as *La Habana Vieja* or Old Havana. The door and windows were kept shut to keep out the street noise and pollution. Since Manolo and his wife had no children, no pets, and no plants, and the house itself was old and musty, it was hard to look forward to going there, except for the great kindness that I perceived in my uncle's bespectacled eyes, and the unquestionable pleasure my father derived from seeing him.

I don't remember ever having a conversation with my uncle during all those years. As soon as we arrived for our afternoon visit, my sister and I would be entrusted to my uncle's wife and her mother. Tía Isabelita was a nurse, a very thin and nervous woman, who would exclaim as we arrived, *"¡Pobrecito!"* *"¡Pobrecita!,"* "Poor dear ones!"—implying that we must have had a long and tiring journey. Then she would pat my little sister gently on the head, exclaiming, *"¡Qué bonita, pobrecita!"* as though being pretty was something to be sad about.

Her mother was a country woman from northern Spain. She was a large, kind woman with a sad smile and teary eyes, who would bring us milk and cookies, and more cookies, and more milk, as if feeding us was her only way of telling us she cared.

I was a little intimidated by both of them, and wished that they would ask me questions the way other adults did, instead of pressing more milk and cookies on me.

Meanwhile, my mother and father carried on what I imagined to be a fascinating conversation with my uncle. The topic always seemed to be politics, and I tried to listen, although I could hardly make out the words over the sighs of my aunt and her mother, exclaiming for the hundredth time that my braids were so much longer than the previous year.

I don't know why I felt that the conversations with my uncle were so important. They certainly seemed to be so for my father, who looked invigorated by them. And I always wondered why we spent so much time with my mother's family and so little time with my father's.

More surprising to me still was that among my mother and

her sisters, my uncle Manolo—so serious, so dignified behind his round tortoiseshell glasses—was spoken of in the same tone that my *tía* Isabelita used when she called my sister and me *"¡Pobrecitas!"*

"They never travel," my aunts would comment, with the self-assurance of having visited Florida and New York themselves.

"They never go anywhere," they would add. "All they do is work and stay in that horrible house."

And then someone would make the comment that silenced everyone, as though there was nothing more that could be said: "And to have chosen to not have children!"

At this point, someone would usually glance in my direction. As the oldest child present, I might be starting to catch on to things. The speaker would be hushed with a vague comment, "Well, considering . . ."

A shadow of mystery hung over it all. A shadow easily forgotten on the many exciting days during those trips to La Habana: a visit to the newly constructed zoo, with the beautiful statue of a deer at the front gate; evening strolls along the *Malecón,* the promenade along the ocean, watching huge waves crashing and turning into cascades of foam while we licked ice-cream cones in fabulous island flavors—coconut, mango, *guanábana, níspero.* There were wonderful days at the beach, at nearby Santa María del Mar, in Guanabo, or even farther away in Varadero, with its incomparable sand.

There were excursions by ferry to El Morro Castle, the old

Spanish fortress on the other side of the bay. Here we could see the impressive stone walls, thick and imposing, built to withstand the cannons of pirate ships and of the British navy. There were turrets to climb, and dungeons that made us gasp, and deep inside of us the proud secret that my own *abuelito* Medardo had been imprisoned here for having denounced the dictator Machado's tyranny in his newspaper. At that time, no one had told me yet that the terrible imprisonment had destroyed his health. Everyone wanted to forget and, even more, to keep the children from knowing that he had suffered torture and hunger. So I simply gloried quietly in the secret of his heroism.

And then at last it was time for good-byes to aunts, uncles, and cousins, and the long train or bus ride home through valleys studded with royal palms, proudly waving their *pencas,* their fronds, in the wind.

On one occasion, my mother and my sister left earlier, driving home in tía Mireya's car. My father and I stayed behind to return home on the train. He had some business to finish in the old center of town. As usual, as we walked, he urged me to look up and observe the elaborate facades of buildings decorated with fabulous statues, cornices, and cornucopias, now soiled by smog and dust and sometimes obscured by neon signs and political advertisements.

After my father finished his errands, he suggested that we visit his own aunt and uncle. Since I had never heard them mentioned before, this came as a surprise to me. I was excited because everything I did with my father—from trips to the countryside to stargazing—was always filled with revelations.

My father's *tía* Isela and her husband lived out of town. As we waited on a busy corner, watching one overcrowded bus after another pass without stopping, my father began to tell me about his aunt Isela and her husband. In the process, he revealed the mystery of my uncle Manolo.

"My aunt and uncle never had any children of their own," my father began. "My aunt, my mother's younger sister, had lived with us when my brothers and I were little. She loved children and missed having a child around the house. So they decided to adopt a little girl from the *Casa de Beneficencia*."

I knew this old orphanage, which stood on Calle Belascoaín, right across from tía Mireya's house. Since my aunt lived on the third floor, I had often watched from the balcony the children playing in the large courtyard of the old building.

My father continued, "All went well for a few years. They loved the little girl as their very own, and were very happy to have her. But when she became a teenager, something terrible happened."

His voice became very sad, and I waited expectantly. Just then a bus stopped, and a large group of people got off. We crowded our way in, my father protecting me with his out-stretched arms. For quite a few blocks we rode standing up, squeezed in among so many bodies. But as the bus moved farther away from the city, my father was able to steer us to the rear, where we finally managed to sit down.

I could not wait to ask him, "What happened that was so terrible?"

"What happened," he answered me, "is that they discovered that the girl had a terrible, terrible illness.

"It is an old disease that humans have known for a very long time. It has always been thought to be incurable, and even worse, highly contagious. It is an illness called leprosy."

I was puzzled when I heard the word. I had heard it before, but I had always thought of it as happening in faraway places, or at least in faraway times. I had read about Rodrigo Díaz de Vivar ("El Cid"), the brave Castilian knight who fought against the Moors, who had conquered most of Spain. A legend told that Rodrigo, who was always so just that his own enemies had given him the name *Mío Cid,* "My Lord," had once taken off his gauntlet to shake the hand of a leper. Many considered this the bravest of his deeds. In my own hometown there was a legend about the old lepers' home, *Asilo de San Lázaro,* which was still standing. But now only homeless elders lived there, and I had thought that there was no leprosy left in Cuba.

"How horrible!" was all I could say.

"Yes," agreed my father, and he continued. "They did not know what to do. The medical doctors told them not only that there was no hope for a cure, but that by law she needed to be hospitalized.

"It was very difficult for them to part with the girl they had loved so much. So they moved to where they now live. Their house is right across from the lepers' hospital.

"Visits to the hospital are rather restricted. But living across the road, my aunt could talk to her daughter through the fence, see her in the yard playing or talking with other girls. And she could bring her food from home, her favorite fruits, a special dessert.

"The director and the hospital staff were touched by such devotion. Many relatives of lepers push them out of their minds once they are institutionalized. The longer the lepers are in the hospital, the fewer visits they receive.

"The doctors were also very careful to warn my aunt of the probabilities of contracting the disease. My aunt simply reminded them that they were taking even greater risks. Impressed by her courage and devotion, they opened their doors to her. She could come any day, at any time.

"And she did. She became the confidante of the girls. She listened to their sadness, their anger, their pain, and their dreams. She talked to the young men, to the older patients, and became their friend. She kept track of birthdays and brought home-made delicacies to be shared by all whose birthdays fell in the same month. She donated her own radio, since she was never home to listen to it anyway, and listening to the radio became one of the few pleasures they all could share. She collected old magazines and day-old newspapers for them, although the people who lived close to the hospital had very little to spare, themselves.

"But it was probably her smiles, her words, and the fact that she saw them as the people they were, not as sick people, that made them love her so much.

"No matter how much the leprosy began to deform and destroy her daughter's body, she always talked about her beauty, because she could truly see past the sick body to the person she so dearly loved."

I was listening spellbound when the story took a surprising turn.

"My brother Manolo," my father added, "had always wanted to be a doctor. When our mother got sick and died, his decision was confirmed. As soon as he finished high school at the Instituto in Camagüey, he asked my father to let him apply to the Universidad de La Habana.

"He went to live in a boarding house in El Vedado, near the university, and concentrated very hard on his studies. Feeling homesick for family, he searched out our *tía* Isela. In the years since our mother's death, our aunt had always sent us letters at Christmas and on our birthdays. She always sent regards from her daughter and told us what a beautiful and sensitive person she was. I even suspect that on his first visit, my brother Manolo was not only hoping to see our aunt whom he had not seen in a long time, but also to meet this lovely cousin.

"At first he was appalled to discover what my aunt had not

been willing to reveal in her letters. He confessed to me that nothing in medical school had prepared him for the deformity and pain he saw on his first visit to the leper's hospital. But after that first visit, he could not stop thinking about it. 'I now know,' he told my aunt and her husband on his next visit, 'why I truly wanted to become a doctor. And I know where I will practice.'

"They listened with love and understanding, neither encouraging nor discouraging him. And he did not mention it again. But on the few occasions Manolo went out with a girl, he would let her know of his plans. Some tried to talk him out of it, others laughed nervously and refused to go out with him again.

"So he decided he would never get married. But a nurse in the Hospital Calixto García, where the medical students did their internships, had noticed the bright, quiet student. She was a little older than he, but so slightly built that she looked younger than her years. When they met for an occasional cup of coffee, usually on the nights he was on duty and after she had finished her shift, she would ask him about his plans and listen as he talked about the lepers, their pain, their isolation, their abandonment.

"Finally she asked him once, 'When are you going there next?' And when he told her, she asked to go with him. So Manolo and Isabel's first date was a visit to the leper's hospital," my father said, almost as if explaining it to himself. "On the way home, he asked if she would marry him and she accepted.

'Provided that we agree not to have children. I could not bear the fear of passing this illness to a child. Let the patients be our children.'"

And so at last I learned the secret that made people hush every time they talked about my uncle Manolo and my aunt Isabel. My aunt and uncle were not lively and witty, funny and spirited like my mother's family, but their reserved exteriors concealed extraordinarily open and giving hearts.

Chapter 9
The Legend of the White Vulture

The lush Cuban landscape

The quiet streets of present-day Camagüey

THE OLD HOUSE in which I was born, La Quinta Simoni, and the tiny house next to it where my great-grandmother lived were the last two houses on the Calle General Gómez, just before the road reached the river Tínima. On the banks of the river stood the radio station *La Voz del Tínima,* owned by my grandfather Modesto, and a tall bridge spanned the gorge below.

One could spend hours looking down at the river from the bridge, as I often did, watching the ducks dive for food or glide swiftly and gracefully across the water. I observed the herds of goats, black on white, white on black, grazing along the riverbank. On the other side of the river was the smithy, where sweaty men wearing leather aprons shaped horseshoe after horseshoe, or held between their knees the folded leg of the horse they were shoeing.

Walking beyond the bridge, one found a few scattered houses; a corner grocery store; the *Cuartel Agramonte;* the military barracks; and finally, two institutions: an orphanage for boys and a home for elderly people, the *Asilo de San Lázaro.* Formerly, this had been a house for lepers, around which had grown a legend beautifully recorded by our own Tula.

Tula was Gertrudis Gómez de Avellaneda, an idol for some of us growing up in Camagüey. Born in 1814 in Santa María del Puerto de Príncipe, which later became Camagüey, she moved to Spain as a young woman when her widowed mother married a Spaniard. In Madrid, she published poetry, plays, and an abolitionist novel, and became one of the literary giants of the Romantic period. She never forgot Cuba, and her love for the island of proud royal palms appears over and over throughout her work. Later in life, she returned to visit her homeland. It was very exciting to me to have been born in the same town as this great woman writer.

Her legend of the white vulture, *el aura blanca,* fascinated me because I knew the places she was describing, which truly had not changed very much in the past hundred years. Yes, now there were cars, electricity, and telephones, but essentially it was still a very quiet town, where most people knew each other, where stores closed at midday so that people could rest during *siesta* time, where the same festivities were held year after year, and where some still had plenty while others begged on the streets.

One thing that *had* changed was that there were no lepers living at the *Asilo de San Lázaro* any longer; now only old people lived there. Compared to those who begged for pennies on the streets, these residents seemed well taken care of, despite how lonely they looked.

The *Asilo de San Lázaro* had originally been founded by

a well-meaning priest, Padre Valencia, to make a home for the numerous lepers who roamed the outskirts of the city. This generous man gave his life to the lepers, both ministering to them and begging on their behalf. He was an eloquent speaker, and his heart was so touched by the pain of those he served that he managed to touch the hearts of others. Whenever he preached in town, he was able to collect the money that allowed him to build, slowly but steadily, his *asilo*.

Padre Valencia spent nothing on himself. To strengthen his own spirit, he practiced the life of an ascetic, sleeping on two boards supported by a few bricks on the floor, with another brick as a pillow.

Daily he would walk through the town, knocking on doors, asking for charity for the lepers. And while he lived, the lepers lacked nothing. But even holy men die. After a long life of caring for others, Padre Valencia passed away.

Other priests took over his role, but they did not possess Padre Valencia's eloquence, nor his determination to walk the streets. And so the alms diminished and all but disappeared. Finally, convinced that it was impossible to keep the *asilo* going, the priests departed as well. Only the lepers remained— the hungry, abandoned lepers.

And then one morning, as the unfortunate men and women gathered sadly in the courtyard to contemplate another day of misery, a surprising bird landed in their midst.

Cuba has an abundance of vultures, known as *auras*. They

can be seen on almost any day, soaring high, enormous wings spread wide, ebony black against the sky, searching for the dead animals on which they feed.

People know these birds are useful, since as scavengers they help keep the countryside clean. And while close-up they are not exactly beautiful, up in the sky they are quite majestic.

The large bird that appeared among the lepers was indeed an *aura.* But two things were most surprising: First, it had descended among them with no apparent fear, a very unusual behavior. And the second was that this *aura,* unlike the ones seen frequently in the sky, was completely white.

"A miracle! A miracle!" the lepers cried. "Just as I was thinking of Padre Valencia," volunteered one. "Just as I was praying to him to not abandon us," another added.

And although the *asilo* was far from town, the news spread immediately. Farmers passing by on their way to market took the amazing news with them. And people who would never have thought of visiting the *asilo* now could not be held back. *¡Un aura blanca!* No one had ever seen one before.

So they went to see the bird, for which the lepers had built a simple cage. And they were reminded of Padre Valencia, whose forgotten words of charity and compassion were reawakened in their minds. They were moved by the lepers, who hung back in order to allow people to admire the bird. And donations began to flow once more.

The *aura blanca* lived for several years. People wondered

if it was simply an albino bird and argued why none had ever been seen before or after.

To the lepers, the bird offered inspiration and comfort. Those who had known Padre Valencia felt his presence among them and drew courage and strength from his memory. They knew that beyond their sick bodies, something bright and luminous would always exist. Those who had not previously known Padre Valencia now learned about him and, seeing their fellow sufferers inspired, were inspired as well.

When the *aura* died, it was embalmed and taken on tour throughout the island. Donations flowed to the lepers from wherever the *aura* went.

Years later, the government centralized the treatment of people with leprosy. The *Asilo de San Lázaro* was renamed *Asilo Padre Valencia* and was turned over to the care of old people. Yet we still used the old name, names being hard to change in a traditional town like Camagüey. And Padre Valencia's sleeping cell remained intact. One could still see the narrow boards he had once used for a bed, the brick on which he had rested his tired head, and, on a wooden perch, the embalmed body of the mysterious *aura blanca*.

Chapter 10

Storm!

The family on the porch of La Quintica

La Quintica, built by my father in 1950

Every morning, when I was a very young child, my *abuelita* would come silently into my room while I was still sleeping. I would wake up in her arms, fragrant with ylang-ylang, which she gathered from a large tree by the entrance of the house and then dried to put in all her drawers. She would help me dress and then take me by the hand to go see the cows and to drink a glass of fresh and foamy milk.

The best cow, the one with the creamiest and most abundant milk, was called Lolita, just like abuelita. No one considered this disrespectful. It was common to give a cow its owner's name.

But when I was eight years old, we moved to the city after my uncle's death and all the cows were sold. After living in the city for a few years, we returned to live in La Quintica, a very small house by the river, that my father built with his own hands. The big house was too large; now that the family had dispersed, we could not afford to keep it up on our own, so it was leased out to a trucking company. Then one of my mother's cousins who had a farm gave us a cow. The cow was allowed to roam freely in a pasture on the other side of the river. Once a day, a neighboring farmer milked her for us.

My mother named the cow Matilde, in honor of her cousin's wife. It was a black cow with white spots, and from the day she arrived we never lacked fresh milk. The milk was so rich, we saved the cream to make our own butter.

Every day, I placed the cream in the refrigerator. Once a week, I gathered it in a bowl and stirred it over and over again with a wooden spoon. As it grew harder, I placed ice cubes in the bowl and continued to stir. Then I washed the hardened cream several times with cold water. The first few times, the water was milky, but I kept on washing until the water was completely clear and the cool butter was resting on the bottom of the bowl, ready to be sprinkled with salt and spread on the freshly baked bread the baker had just brought in.

When the cow Matilde was going to have a calf, we could not agree on what the calf's name would be. Felipe, after my mother's cousin? Lolita, after my grandmother's favorite cow?

One night, we woke up startled by the sound of thunder. Lightning had struck close to the house, which shook as if hit by an explosion. My father said he thought he heard Matilde mooing in distress.

None of us heard anything except the cracks of thunder and the drumming rain. But my father, always proud of his good hearing, put on his raincoat and walked out into the torrent falling from the sky. The fading light from his large flashlight signaled to us that he had gone toward the wooden bridge. With the heavy rain, the river would be too full to ford at the crossing. My mother and I stayed up waiting for him. She warmed some milk on the stove and put some water to boil to make fresh coffee. Very soon, its strong aroma filled the house.

I accepted a cup of warm milk with some drops of dark coffee, and soon fell asleep on the couch. When the thunder woke me again, my mother was on the porch. I joined her just at the moment a gust of wind sent a sheet of rain against the house, soaking us. But my mother refused to go back in, searching in the darkness for some sign of my father.

All of a sudden, a flash of lightning outlined the shape of what looked to be a horrible monster. Although shorter than a man, it had a monstrous head that made me think of the Minotaur in one of my grandmother's books of mythology. I shook with fear.

My mother instead ran toward the shadowy figure that was approaching our porch. Not knowing very well what to do, I followed her. Right then, another flash of lightning illuminated the night. As though struck by the bolt, the monster seemed to split in two as my father took the newborn calf that he had been carrying on his shoulders and placed it on its wobbling legs. Matilde, who had followed my father and her calf through the storm, stood nearby.

"What about calling it *Temporal*?" my father asked as he shook out his jacket. My mother laughed. Unquestionably, *Temporal,* the Spanish word for "tropical storm," was a perfect name. My mother continued to laugh as she tried to dry the rainwater from my father's face. They both went in the house.

I stayed outside, soaking wet, watching Matilde lick her newborn calf as though the rain, which had become softer and softer, were not enough to clean him.

Epilogue

My father, sister, me, and my mother

LIFE IN OUR OLD colonial city had a very special flavor. Time seemed to move very slowly, as each day repeated the previous one. Any experience outside the ordinary received an enormous amount of attention and became the focus of everyone's conversation for many days to come.

For a small child eager to understand life, my surroundings provided a wealth of information just from observing how people behaved. It was surprising that among a relatively small number of people there could be so much diversity—each person constituting a world of her own, of his own.

Today, many years later, from a great distance in both time and space, I find that much of what I learned back then is still fresh in my memory and continues to inform my understanding of life and its mysteries.

May these stories help you see the richness all around you . . . and the richness within you.

Acknowledgments

WRITING A MEMOIR invites reflection. On writing this book, the overwhelming feeling that arises in me is that of gratitude:

Gratitude to my grandparents, parents, aunts, and uncles, who nurtured my childhood with their love and enriched it with their example and their stories.

Gratitude to my children: Rosalma, Alfonso, Miguel, and Gabriel Zubizarreta, who have been a constant source of inspiration for my creativity and of support in all aspects of my life.

Gratitude to Isabel Campoy for her caring presence and for bringing joy and beauty to the journey.

To my grandchildren, who are a source of renewed hope.

To all of my students, who throughout my half century of teaching have allowed me to learn alongside them and to see life through their eyes.

To librarians and teachers, for your daily work in facilitating the "magical encounter" between books and readers. May you continue to see your efforts blossom.

To Emma Ledbetter for her careful shepherding of this project. I could not have had a better editor. It has been a real pleasure to work with you!

And to all of the wonderful Atheneum family. During the delightful process of publishing seventeen different titles with you during the last seventeen years, I have felt supported and encouraged by everyone in the production team, from publishers to copyeditors.

It takes many minds and hands to make a book come to life, and I thank you all: Justin Chanda, publisher, for your kind enthusiasm in receiving this book as well as earlier ones; Clare McGlade, production editor, for helping the book take final form; Lauren Rille, designer, for having found a way to combine all of the various elements of this book in a graceful format; Tom Finnegan, copyeditor, for helping catch the elusive and mischievous typos; and Elizabeth Blake-Linn for turning the digital file into a tangible book.

I also thank those of you who help make the books known to libraries and schools, especially Michelle Leo and Candace Greene-McManus.

Special recognition is due to my daughter Rosalma, who patiently reviewed each line of this book to help me say exactly what I meant to say, in the way I had wanted to say it. I value each moment we have spent together in shaping and reshaping sentences. My admiration and love for you continue to grow as I rejoice in witnessing your own growth.

Words, Phrases, and Expressions:
Spanish to English Glossary

Some words have multiple meanings. The meaning listed here corresponds to the one used in the context of this book.

abuelita: grandma

abuelito: grandpa

alfarero: brick and roof-tile maker

afilador: a person who sharpens knives and other blades

algarrobo: saman or rain tree, a large tree native to Mexico, the Caribbean, and the northern part of South America

aljibe: underground water deposit

ambrosía: ambrosia, the legendary food of the Olympian gods and goddesses

anón, anones: a tropical fruit of the sugar apple or custard apple family, which also includes *chirimoya* and *guanábana*

arroz con leche: rice pudding

asilo: a charitable house for orphans or elderly people

ateje: a tree originally from Cuba, whose wood is used for artistic carvings, and whose red berries are a favorite food for hens

aura: a Cuban species of vulture, with black feathers and a bald head, that feeds on dead animals

aura blanca: a very rare form of an *aura*, born as an albino (all white)

¡Ayúdalo, Papá!: Help him, Daddy!

azotea: accessible flat rooftop

bañarnos en el aguacero: literally "to take a bath in the rain;" in the story
    context, running around under light rain dressed in a bathing suit

barquillero: street seller of *barquillos*

barquillos: thin rolled wafers

barrilete, barriletes: kite, kites

biajaca: a type of fish native to Cuban rivers

bisabuela: great-grandmother

bohío: a thatched house designed originally by the indigenous people
    of the Caribbean

bongó: a type of Caribbean drum made of wood with a goatskin
    drumhead

boniatos: sweet potatoes

botijo: a clay vessel for water. Its rounded body has a handle on top,
    and two openings: one to pour in the water, the other to drink
    from. Synonym of *porrón,* which is the preferred word in Cuba

Buenos días: good morning

café con leche: warm milk mixed with a small portion of strong
    coffee

caimito, caimitos: this tropical fruit is known by various names: star
    apple, golden leaf tree, *abiaba*, milk fruit

calabaza: pumpkin

calabozo: dungeon

calentito: "nice and warm"

campesinos: farm workers

camposanto: holy ground, cemetery

candelita: small fire

canutillo: a plant that grows on the banks of rivers and creeks, and has long, tender leaves that chickens love to eat

carolinas, árbol de carolina: a magnificent tropical tree. Once a year, it loses all of its leaves and becomes covered with long brown flower buds that resemble cigars. When the buds open, they reveal either white or red flowers, which do not have petals but have a crown of multiple pistils.

carriola: a child's scooter, consisting of two wheels with a low footboard between them. It has a handlebar to steer with, and you ride it by resting one foot on the footboard while using your other foot to push against the ground.

casera, caserita: housewife ("*caserita*" is more endearing)

ceiba: kapok tree

chirimoya: a tropical fruit of the sugar apple or custard apple family, which also includes *anón* and *guanábana*

coco, cocos: coconut, coconuts

coquitos acaramelados: ground coconut balls covered in a caramel candy coating

comparsa: a group of people who celebrate Carnival by participating in a parade with matching costumes. They dance to the beat of the drums and sometimes carry *farolas*.

conga: in Cuba, a group of people who celebrate Carnival by dancing in the streets to the rhythm of music of African origin, played on various kinds of percussion instruments. Also the name of a specific dance and of a specific drum

conserva de guayaba: guava paste

cuchillo de mango blanco: knife with a white bone handle

dulce: sweet or sweet dessert

dulce de coco: coconut dessert

dulce de leche: caramelized milk dessert

dulcero: seller of sweets

empanadilla: a type of meat or fruit pocket pie, similar to a Cornish pasty

empanadillero: seller of *empanadillas*

farolas: decorated poles with a lantern on top, carried by the members of a *comparsa*

Fiesta de San Juan: Saint John's Feast Day, June 24

¡Frijolito!: "Beany!" shouted in defiance during Carnival to men dressed as *mono viejos,* trying to frighten children

fritas: small, spicy hamburger

framboyanes: flame trees

gavetita: little drawer

goma arábiga: Gum Arabic or acacia gum, a hardened sap used to make glue

guajacones: Cuban freshwater minnows

guajira: a musical composition popular in the Cuban countryside, where the farmers are called *guajiros*

guanábana: Caribbean tree and fruit. The fruit pulp is white, sweet, and very refreshing.

guano: species of small palm tree used for thatching *bohíos*

guayaba: guava

guayabera: a lightweight shirt designed to be worn untucked, with two vertical rows of fine, tiny, pleats running down the front and back. There is a sports version with short sleeves, as well as a long-sleeved dress version that can be worn with a bow tie instead of a coat and tie.

guayabos: guava trees

güienes: reeds

habanera: a Cuban dance in slow duple meter, with a rhythm similar to that of a tango

hacienda: cattle ranch and farm

heladero: street vendor of ice cream

helado: ice cream

horno de carbón: furnace to make coal

jicoteas: Cuban river turtles

malanga blanquita: very white taro root

mamarrachos: a Carnival costume with no particular characteristic except making the bearer unrecognizable

mangos de hilacha: a species of mango that is very stringy. Typically this mango is eaten by first pounding on it and then squeezing out its juice, since otherwise the high fiber content makes its pulp difficult to chew and swallow.

mangos de mamey: a delicious species of mango with a sweet pulpy meat and little fiber

mangos del Caney: the mangoes from the region of El Caney, close to Santiago de Cuba, which have the reputation of being the best mangoes in Cuba

maní, maníes: peanut, peanuts

manisero: seller of roasted peanuts

manzana del coco: coconut apple, the flavorful soft ball of the coconut meat formed within the coconut when it is ready to sprout

marabú: a wild and invasive plant, also known as "sickle bush"

maravillas: bushes with multicolored flowers that are closed during the day and open at night

marañón: cashew tree or cashew fruit

mi: my, as in *mi abuelita*, my grandmother; *mi bisabuela*, my great-grandmother

mono viejo: a particular Carnival costume worn by men, made of colorful, flowery material that covers the whole body except the eyes, and has dozens of jingle bells attached. An essential part of the costume is the long, heavy tail, used to threaten to whip those who get too close!

masa: dough, either of wheat flour or cornmeal

ñame: edible white root, a kind of yam, similar to—but different from—cassava

néctar: legendary drink of the gods and goddesses of Olympus

niña: girl

níspero: fruit native to Southern Mexico, Central America, and the Caribbean. The tree can be very large. The fruit has a coarse brown skin; the flesh varies in color from pale yellow to rose and has an exceptionally sweet, malty flavor. While, in Spain, *"níspero"* refers to the loquat fruit, the Latin-American *níspero* (also called *sapodilla* or *chicozapote*) is an altogether unrelated fruit.

nostalgia: profound homesickness or longing

pan: bread

pan de leche: milk bread

pan de huevo: egg bread

panadero: baker

papagayos: parrots; the name given to kites in some countries

papalote: kite (from the Nahuatlan word *papalotl,* meaning butterfly)

papas fritas: fried potatoes (french fries)

papel de China: a shiny, translucent, sturdy paper in bright colors, well suited for making kites

paraíso: paradise

pencas: the fronds of palm trees and coconut trees

picante: spicy, hot

piñita Pijuán: a pineapple soft drink (unique to Camagüey, Cuba)

pisa: a round pit where clay is broken and softened by a large iron wheel

plancha: a flat-bed cart pulled by a horse

¡Pobrecito! ¡Pobrecita!: "Poor dear one!" (an affectionate expression)

por favor: please

porrón: a clay vessel for water. Its rounded body has a handle on top and two openings, one to pour in the water, the other to drink from. A synonym is *botijo.*

puré de papas: mashed potatoes

¡Qué bonita, pobrecita!: "How beautiful, the poor dear one!"

ranas toro: bullfrogs

renacuajos: tadpoles

Reyes Magos: the Three Wise Men—Melchior, Gaspar, and

Balthazar—who, according to the Gospels, brought gifts to the
baby Jesus. In Spanish-speaking countries, children tradition-
ally received their Christmas gifts on the morning of January
6th, the feast day dedicated to the *Reyes Magos*. Sadly, with the
globalization of Santa Claus, this tradition has been changing.

rumba: a lively Afro-Caribbean dance

saleta: an informal living room, distinct from the more formal *sala*

señora: lady

siboney, siboneyes: indigenous people of Cuba

siesta: the period of time in the early afternoon where people tradi-
tionally take a brief rest after lunch

taburete: a sturdy chair with the seat and back made of cowhide

tamal, tamales: a cornmeal dough with pork, chicken, chilies, or
other ingredients inside, wrapped in a corn husk

tamalero: seller of *tamales*

tamarindo: tamarind, a bittersweet tropical fruit

tejar: a place where bricks and clay tiles, or *tejas,* are made

tejas: clay roof tiles

temporal: tropical storm

tía: aunt

tierna: tender

tinajón: a very large rounded clay vessel, sometimes up to six feet
high. It was used in colonial times throughout Camagüey to
store water and has become the symbol of the city of Camagüey.
The plural is *tinajones*.

tinajoncito: a very small replica of a *tinajón,* used as a souvenir *tío*: uncle

tranvías: electric trolley cars

tumbadoras: a specific form of Caribbean drums

viandas: edible root vegetables

viandero: a seller of *viandas*

ylang-ylang: also called ilang-ilang, fragrant cananga, Macassar-oil plant, or perfume tree, this tropical tree originally from the Philippines is highly valued for its perfume. The small yellow flowers can be dried and placed where linens and clothes are stored to impart their fragrance.

yuca: cassava, an edible root

People Mentioned in This Book

Maternal family

Alma Lafuente Salvador - Mamá, mother

Flor Alma Ada Lafuente - Florecita, sister

Medardo Lafuente Rubio - abuelito Medardo, grandfather

Dolores (Lola) Salvador Méndez - abuelita Lola, *mi paraíso*, grandmother

Federico Salvador Arias - great-grandfather

Marcelina (Mina) Méndez Correoso - bisabuela Mina, great-grandmother

Genoveva Méndez Correoso - great-grandmother's sister

Virginia Lafuente Salvador - tía Virginia, aunt

Virginita - cousin, tía Virginia's daughter

Jorge - cousin, tía Virginia's son

Mireya Lafuente Salvador - tía Mireya, aunt

Medardo (Medardito) Lafuente Salvador - tío Medardito, uncle

Geraldina - aunt, Medardito's wife

Nancy - cousin, Medardito and Geraldina's daughter

Lolita Lafuente Salvador - tía Lolita, aunt

Manolo Díaz - tío Tony, tía Lolita's husband

Mireyita - cousin, tía Lolita and tío Tony's daughter

Paternal family
Modesto Ada Rey - Papá, father
Modesto Ada Barral - abuelito Modesto, grandfather
María Rey Paz - grandmother
Isela Rey Paz - great-aunt
Manuel (Manolo) Ada Rey - tío Manolo, uncle
Isabel - tía Isabelita, tío Manolo's wife
Mario - tío Mario, uncle

Other people mentioned
Ignacio Agramonte - Cuban patriot
Amalia Simoni - Ignacio Agramonte's wife
Félix Caballero - surveyor, friend of Modesto Ada Rey
Samoné - worker
Emilio Pimentel - caretaker
Zenaida - circus girl
Gladys Carnero - teacher, Colegio Episcopal de San Pablo
Gilda Zaldívar - ballet teacher
Coralia - my mother's former nanny
Mr. Charles - French professor
Madame Marie - lady who was a French Jewish refugee